A Boro Boy -
Connections with Nature

C000165606

Joshua McGowan

2QT (Publishing) Ltd

First Edition published 2021 by
2QT Limited (Publishing)
Settle, North Yorkshire BD24 9RH United Kingdom

Photograph P129 - © Tom Parker
All other internal photographs: © Joshua McGowan
Cover Image from original photograph: © Kay Webb
Illustrations: Emmy Turner Art

Printed in Great Britain by IngramSparks

A CIP catalogue record for this book is available
from the British Library

ISBN - 978-1-913071-95-0

Contents

Preface

Muse
Verb: to think about something carefully and for a long time.

This collection of thoughts and stories expresses my ever-growing obsession with wildlife, which started when I was very young. Luckily for me, I have an amazing, supportive family who have always encouraged me and helped my passion for the great outdoors to blossom.
My very first interests were exotic mammals and birds; however, as I have grown older, I have started to favour simpler things and truly appreciate the beautiful nature that is all around us.

   I have never been an organised person when it comes to writing about my experiences. I have multiple notebooks on the go, crammed with little facts that I have picked up along the way. I decided to gather these scattered findings into one neatly organised document, and that has become the book that you are reading.

   I have really connected with my senses and, through them, to nature. I've always been fascinated by it and wanted to research every detail I came across. My stories are pieces of a jigsaw that I want to share with you.

   If you were not fortunate enough to have the oppor-

1

tunity to enjoy nature when you were growing up, or even during the later stages of your life, you might not appreciate certain parts of the natural world. Perhaps this book will remind you how to reconnect with it.

It is only when you sit back and relax that you realise your life experiences are precious. It is then that you connect with your memories, to nature and the comfort it offers. Once the mind is left to roam, it can really find what is precious.

I did not appreciate my childhood in the north-east of England until, as a teenager, I opened my eyes to its history, our family connection to it and my love for local wildlife. For a long time I was not interested in much else. My ambition was to explore, learn and plug into the natural world – and that inspired me to become a zookeeper.

I was born and bred in Middlesbrough and, helped by my encouraging family, my childhood was constantly shared with nature. I have moved around the UK and enjoyed different parts of it; hopefully there will be more to come as I venture in search of more connections and experiences.

When things are looking bleak and all you read about is destruction across the globe, just show a bit of love for nature and you will reap the benefits.

Joshua McGowan
August 2020

Stepping into another world of the reed beds. Showing off my waders and slimy mud up my arms and face. Happy.

Introduction

I WANT TO start by thanking you for purchasing my very first book.

I love to be surrounded by natural life; to me it is a place of safety and comfort. Our brains have evolved around the natural landscape; scientists agree that the beauty of nature and being close to the natural world can make you feel healthier. It stimulates positive chemicals that stop you feeling down and can give you an adrenalin buzz. Serotonin and dopamine are given a chance to flow normally, as nature intended. Our modern routines keep our stress levels high and make us feel less healthy; a connection with nature can help with that.

We have been subtly turning our heads away from nature, and advances in technology are making it even easier to ignore. Do we feel grass under our feet – really feel it? Do we accept a decent breeze without turning our head and pulling a face? Are we aware of the scents of nature when we are out walking? Even I sometimes have my head down on a walk as I quickly check my phone. We have come to the point where sometimes we are completely removed from the wild, where only a tiny percent of the population is living outside an adapted man-made environment.

How can we reconnect? Our awareness of nature is still there because it is built into us; it just needs to be engaged. Take a field, for example. Look at its unique history, science, geography, and culture; use your knowledge of the natural world to appreciate it, and protect it by standing up for it.

I talk about being close to nature but it is okay to not want to be surrounded by it all the time. Even I want my comforts sometimes; given the choice, I would not like to spend each night outside. I consider my pillow to be my luxury. But I do like a dawn chorus, or a late night standing in a garden looking for bats and owls. I spend a lot of time away from home because of my work and I often find new, interesting places to sit back and connect with nature. The natural world is the place that has helped me to grow as a person.

At the time of writing, a report has been produced reviewing the UK National Parks and Areas of Outstanding Natural Beauty (AONB), which are continuing to lose biodiversity. These places often use recreation as a marker for their success. I understand that there is less interaction with, and funding for, them and this is stretching the effectiveness of these areas. The decline of national biodiversity is dramatic and it is all around us. My stories focus on two of the national parks where I would love to see an increased contribution from both the government and the general public. These places have been crucial in my personal development.

People go outside but forget about their connection with the world: if you don't feel involved with it, you will miss the point and move on too quickly. It is easy to connect with the countryside when you are in a different landscape to your familiar one because you are more aware of your surroundings. However, it is equally easy to connect with a familiar place like your garden, the local park or nature reserve.

My interests are birds and mammals, and I watch and listen to them constantly wherever I am. My first reaction to most things is to listen and identify the species and what they are trying to communicate.

Nature is being pushed out of mainstream society. I encourage you to get outside and put away technology for a while, or use it in a different way to engage with nature. Technology can help us to connect, for example by using photography to identify species.

We need to reclaim our connection with nature when everything around us is changing and evolving. If we don't, it will soon be too late and we will be asking where all the wildlife went. Why didn't we appreciate its value and protect it in time? Why are the Sumatran tigers all gone? The Spectacled Andean bear? These will be the questions of a seven-year-old growing up, one hundred years in the future.

This is nothing new; many of us, as we mature, ask what we have come to. Can we collectively change our ways? Can we make Fairtrade and other brands better options than basic, cheaper options for most people rather than just a few? The connection we have had with animals and landscapes for thousands of years has changed, been blocked off, maybe now we need to integrate it back into society.

My time outside far outweighs my time inside in making me happy. I constantly think about seeing nature and how I can be involved with it. But we are not all the same. I recently watched someone in a neighbouring garden cut down a row of small ash trees on the boundary of his perfectly square garden. To me, these trees offered privacy and a tool to suck up a bit of local air pollution; someone else saw them as invading their space.

I will always defend the spaces I love. I have written to councils, signed petitions and volunteered over the past decade, and I hope to continue doing so in the future. Many of my stories tell of my appreciation of nature and reflect on points in my life where it has been a big influence.

·•·

I started to think about my experiences with animals at work, and to explore the connection of animals to humans. I wanted to spread the message about how amazing these animals are, and why we need to help and conserve them. Initially, I used to show off the animals that people had paid money to see. I saw the visitors' reactions and they were genuine; they wanted to see, hear, smell, and feel the animals (though some animals do not want to be touched!).

However, many people are overwhelmed when they encounter animals for the first time and they don't absorb information about them. I started to focus less on giving information and more on explaining their different mannerisms, habits and emotions that we can relate to. This always got an overwhelmingly positive reaction. To understand and connect with a place or animal, we must understand the past and present culture we have shared.

This book is structured around the animals and places that I have experienced. I have tried to explain how certain places and animals surprised me and what each experience meant to me. I write as someone who has learnt as much as I can to get different perspectives on conservation.

Every human action makes a difference to the present and impacts on the future; that, in turn, affects the biodiversity of the United Kingdom and the world. In 2020, the coronavirus pandemic had a grave impact on us all. Many businesses and organisations have been temporarily closed; gyms, cinemas, pubs and shops were forced to shut. This has allowed some of us to get back to basics and make the most of what is on offer in the natural world. Maybe this pandemic has given us a chance to explore the world around us that we have been ignoring for many years.

So get your waders ready, grab a biscuit or two – and breathe. Newts around the corner…

The Earlier Years

IN THE DARK underwater world, we have palmate newts! We had newts settle into the first pond in our home because there were plenty of plants and food on offer. This is a photo from my family garden, where I made my own nature reserves after nearly two decades of care and research. As I pond dipped, I wondered what life was underneath the surface; what do I miss when I walk past every day?

The garden was my first project and my first chance to get into the field of conservation. I never left it alone. I started with the usual bird table, bird bath and nest box, then put in my first pond. That started as a big plastic box filled with pond plants, and I added some 'pond soup', which is a bucket full of life including tadpoles from a nearby pond.

The pond ended up being very successful – with birds using it as a food takeaway! The jays and blackbirds gobbled up the tadpoles. Damn! Despite this, other creatures used the garden and the cycle of life continued.

When the common frog and a species of darter dragonfly moved in, I built a new pond with a pond liner. This was even more successful and was visited by adult frogs, and another species of dragonfly, the chaser. It became a valuable spot for a variety of animals. That was remarkable when you consider that the pond was just a tiny dot in a housing estate.

Looking at indicators of wildlife thriving. A tiny palmate newt and its relatives at home in my ponds.

Roll on a few more years and we moved again. This time I brought some of the pond-water 'soup' from our previous garden in my dad's car. My dad drove very slowly over the bumps and round the corners, as if he were on his driving test. Luckily, our new house was only five minutes' drive away; any more, and the wildlife would have created a car 'pond'. We also transported tree saplings and rocks I had collected from around the country that needed to move with me.

As I grew up, I built more ponds, totalling four. I 'landscaped' the gardens with live traps, drainage systems and tree planting, sometimes without my parents being aware of it.

The most recent garden started with me concentrating on a carnivorous beetle on the dry, dusty soil. How could it get like this – a garden with nothing more than a beetle, grey squirrel and a cat?

I asked myself: What do you see as the end goal; Where do you think the project will be in five years' time? These are common questions in interviews for conservation jobs, especially where the projects involved landscape or species' improvement. This was my early version. I had a vision of hedgerows, trees and predators such as foxes.

⁓

I never liked going to school. I didn't mind seeing my friends, but I didn't do well in my school work. I found simple things difficult because I was not connecting with school education. I wanted to learn about the natural world; the best moments for me were the times we went on school trips to new places, into woodlands or even on the school field.

When I went to secondary school, I realised the importance of improving myself. I found myself in the bottom classes, in groups where the kids didn't care about learning. The chaos they caused shocked me at first; it wasn't in my nature to misbehave or be a bad student, I just wanted to get the day over. I saw these kids and it kicked me into action. I was determined to do the best I could during my time there and to get out of those classes. I worked hard and became the strange teen in school who looked like he wanted to learn.

Away from school I played football and saw my friends, but my focus was the natural world. I acquired hobbies and started to become the person I wanted to be. I am a slow learner but each year, little by little, I inched higher and finally got my grades.

I used the family camcorder for years until, eventually, wear and tear set in. I bought my own small version, which developed my skills, and I researched my new interest – nature photography. My next ambition was to upgrade to something similar to the cameras they use in the BBC Natural History Unit. I couldn't afford the exact stuff but I found a new camcorder using SD cards instead of cassettes, with HD and options for an interchangeable lens with greater zoom and wider camera shots.

I came up with ideas to earn some cash to buy it. I sold home-baked cookies at school, which my mam made for me. Each day was a toss between wanting to eat the cookie and making a few pennies. I reckoned at that rate I could own my own high-spec camcorder within twelve years. Thankfully, I saved up from odd jobs helping around the house, and the camcorder joined me on many of my trips, together with wildlife notes that I made based on the images. Filming was another step for me to record behaviour, cross distances without disturbing the wildlife, play around with settings and get my head used to all these letters and numbers. The world of videography was now on my TV screen and I was raring to go.

Camera at the ready, set to film Red deer in a valley, in Scotland.

Blue Tit 24/7

As STRUCTURED CULTIVATION rose and fell in Roman times, the rich prospered and the taming of the countryside continued with drainage, hunting and destroying pests. Smaller and more flexible species moved in and benefited from the imbalance. Up to 80 per cent of the human population in the United Kingdom now has 'enclosed spaces' in the form of shared or private gardens.

You could be sharing territories with one of the 3.6 million-plus blue tits (*cyanistes caeruleus*); their space is your space. The proliferation of blue tits was helped by the planting style in gardens that developed in the sixteenth century.

Blue tits will often use a crack or an old woodpecker's round hole in a tree as a nest. A nest box is a rectangular wooden box with a hole in the front about a third from the top, just big enough for the parent to squeeze in and out of. It is a popular artificial replica and has proved a successful place for blue tits to raise their young because it helps prevent predators from finding, accessing and stealing the young.

In the nineteenth century, a British man, Charles

Waterton, invented a box for the bird life on the estate he owned. It was a grand example and the idea grew from there. There are now many variations including pigeon lofts, waterfowl huts, martin banks and house brick nests.

─●

My blue tit family had their own wooden real estate on the garage wall. This was a very safe community surrounded by Japanese ivy (*parthenocissus tricuspidata*) and an all-you-can-eat food buffet in the shrubbery nearby. That nest box provided for blue tits for more than a decade and it gave me one of my first important connections with wildlife.

The big bright world and this tiny bird interact for the first time when a fledgling (the term used for baby birds leaving the nest) reaches the hole of the nest box. It sits on the edge of the hole, looking out into the light and visualising the outside environment. Its parents encourage it to leave. They have been popping in and out, providing care for the past fifteen to twenty-one days with each chick eating up to a hundred caterpillars each per day.

Seeing a blue tit move into the outside world is a very special moment, crucial in the little bird's life. Unfortunately, we often miss these important occasions because we are distracted by fast-paced modern life. Many fledgling birds will take the leap of faith early in the morning in the first few hours of daylight when we don't always want to leave the warmth of our bed, preferring to get a little more shut-eye! Luckily we now have nest-box cameras!

Traditionally, the blue tit is thought as a woodland species, but it is opportunistic and will adapt to the spaces we offer, such as gardens with trees, using nest boxes in gardens and parks. The woodland that keeps the wildlife thriving has been hacked away over the centuries, so our gardens have become more important than ever.

The blue tit begins its selection of 'real estate' by looking for ideal features: the positioning of a potential 'home', the chances of being watched over by predators, and the distance of green space from cover. The height of the home off the ground is important, as are north-east facing boxes to offer protection for new residents...

Blue tits are very observant. We spend winter in our warm houses, removed from the cold, while the blue tit is looking for a nest to come out and enjoy our 'shared space'. However, the blue tit doesn't select a nest knowing they are going to be sharing, so they have to adapt and hope our presence is not threatening for them or their family. I call it a shared space because a garden might be paved or covered in lawn, which is less than helpful to the broad range of animals and birds who could use it, including the blue tit.

Because of our milder winters, nest selection can begin in January, followed by nest building and interior design in late February to March (this only works if a cold snap does not intervene). The female blue tit lays a clutch of eggs over several days before incubating them; fifteen days of brooding and incubation is a tough ask.

A blue tit can produce eight to twelve eggs; if eight hatch and the parents are lucky enough to breed a second clutch, that will be sixteen fledglings leaving the nest, and a higher chance that their genes will be passed on successfully to the next generation.

One of my favourite moments is passing a box and hearing the chicks screeching for food as the adult bird returns with a fat green caterpillar. Adults need to find up to as many as one thousand caterpillars every day. No wonder they struggle with climate change if the caterpillars and chicks turn up at different times, with no warning. Also, the markers they rely on emerge at different rates. Leaves, flowers and temperature are very important to the blue tit, much more so than in our world where we have dates and times at our fingertips.

When the chick leaves the nest, it has an increased chance of being eaten up. This fluffy dumpling must adjust quickly to the surrounding environment because the world is full of predators from the moment the parent builds a nest. I have seen woodpeckers peck the front of boxes, weasels pluck out a chick, and magpies and crows steal fledglings off the ground.

The type and location of the nest is crucial for chick survival. Predation can be reduced with a bit of green cover, so a varied garden rather than just a lawn will help the little fledglings and give us time to enjoy more of the blue tits. The natural world needs to be protected and a nest box is an amazing start. Think about how many generations of blue tits can thrive in one nest box placed in the correct position.

My nest box was in full production by May. When I came home, I never wanted to be in the house – what kid would want to miss out on blue tits? Some evenings after school, I set up my camcorder at the side of the garden with the tea tray as my tripod. To hide my body and not scare off the birds, I used my army camouflage tent with netting over me and my equipment. Sometimes the camcorder was already in position; other days I sat on the kitchen worktop watching and waiting.

The blue tit can return to the nest up to fifty times an hour (sometimes up to seventy!). By the time I saw them in the late afternoon, the parents were probably exhausted, having been up since half-past four or five in the morning searching for food both for themselves and the chicks.

Caterpillar numbers may boom in a dry year, but only if their own food source is flourishing and the leaves are emerging with fewer toxins. In wet seasons, the blue tit parents must battle the elements and work hard to find grubs that could be washed away. No wonder blue tits only live for 2.7 years on average. We can help them out a bit in spring by supplying mealworms through the breeding season. Success rates also depend on predation levels, weather patterns and much more.

Blue tit parents have a harder time than most because of the rapid rate of chick development, and they are in a constant loop of collecting caterpillars and feeding the babies. The parents regularly take away faecal sacks (the eco poo bag produced by a chick), eggshells and chicks that do not make it – but even removing a faecal sack burns energy. If they survive these challenges, the next generation will be stronger and more capable of dealing with life around humans.

Before the time of cheap nest-box cameras, I had to wait and hope to get pictures. One warm evening I set up my camcorder and was waiting in the garden, which is hard for a fidget. Suddenly a chick poked its head out of the nest box, calling to get its parents' attention. The parents replied from nearby trees. I had probably already missed the earlier fledglings leaving, as they often go early in the morning. This little fella might have been the last of the brood to leave. It was looking at the world around it, something it had to master quickly in order to survive. It sat for about a minute, chirping away, made the leap – and dropped into the garden.

I was totally involved with the drama. Did this mean the chick had failed? I watched for ten more minutes until eventually the parents came down and fed it. I checked it was in a safe place but didn't interfere with it. The next morning the chick was gone; it could have been eaten by a cat or a rat, though I could hear the blue tit family calling away in the trees.

I had done it: I had managed to film a chick leaving the nest with my camcorder and I had imitated what the team at BBC *Springwatch* had done. I managed to convert the recording to VHS and sent it in to the BBC.

I still get that same smile whenever I see fledglings

pop out. Chances are you'll miss this moment; it can take two minutes or twenty-four hours for the whole brood to fledge, and unless you stay the whole time you will not know their story and feel connected to it.

It is easier now with cheaper cameras. A unit with twenty-four-hour CCTV control inside and outside the box is not common for houses, but if you have it you can have your own live drama outside the nest boxes.

If you have not done this yet, I would recommend giving it a go. Place a nest box with some cover nearby in a north-east facing position, somewhere pesky cats will not interfere! A young blue tit chick comes out of the nest with yellow cheeks and a big yellow smile; that 'gape' is its big mouth that it uses for fitting in lots of meals and getting its parents' attention. As the chick grows, it becomes a small blue and yellow bird characterised by a black eye strip which runs from behind its head through to its beak; distinguishing it from to other tit species in your garden.

I fitted cameras to nest boxes, eager to see the action inside their home. Did the family succeed in getting the eggs to hatch? What was the choice of bedding? It varied depending on what was available in the garden – some years it was moss, pigeon feathers, my dad's cut hair, clothes fibres and leaves. One time the nest was a moss and feather mattress about 5cm thick with a bowl to nestle into; it looked warm and spongy.

The blue tits move around different nests. One of my recent boxes was used for three years before it was abandoned. Since then, I have tried to empty it every other year when the season ends. I clean and disinfect my box to prevent disease and pest build-up, particularly important if the nest is used repeatedly.

One year I peeped in a few weeks after the fledglings left. One of the chicks had failed to leave and was decomposing in the box, surrounded by his new mates – woodlice, earwigs and what I think was the brilliantly named devil's coach horse beetle! Another year my excitement about the baby blue tits was disrupted by wasps that invaded the nest box and created a paperwork entrance. I could not believe how busy it became. My family and our neighbours were soon involved in a war to keep out wasps from the house and the bathroom air vents. As we brushed our teeth, we could hear a buzz and crash above from the occasional lost and confused wasp. I watched the wasps develop their world in the garden before the nest was finally removed. I did have my bird box back for the family of blue tits the next spring, though.

If you think of blue tits, you may think of them targeting bottles of milk and eating the cream. During World War I, milk bottles had a variety of lids including card, wax tops and aluminium foil. Blue tits and other species flew towards the challenge of reaching rich fatty cream. The first recorded example of this came in 1921. Thirty years later, blue tits, great tits and coal tits were still piercing foil tops across the nation.

The clever birds stick to one patch and rarely go far. They've learnt to do this because of their previous success. People have experimented with stones, tea towels and boxes to prevent damage and to limit the 'spoil' of damaged milk. The modern problem for blue tits comes from using plastic cups or milk caps to cover bottles. A drop in doorstep sales also reduced their opportunities. Over the past three decades, home-delivered milk bottles have become rare; old electric milk floats are also rare, even though they are a good idea for reducing food miles. Now consumers tend to buy milk from the shops. Perhaps the enthusiasm for plastic-free produce will see blue tits once again learning the skill of taking cream from milk bottles as they exploit our shared environment.

Millions of birds, including blue tits, help us understand different species in the twenty-first century. Like many species, blue tits are ringed to record data. The oldest blue tit is recorded to have reached fifteen years old!

My hearing is useful in helping me to spot birds. I am always tuned into something, even if it means sacrificing a conversation and saying, 'Sorry, I missed that,' to someone who is speaking to me. Blue tits' communication, like so many species, helps them understand their neighbourhood activity.

The contact call is used by pairs or a parent and chick; this often grabs my attention in May and June when you can hear chicks demanding comfort and a snack. Once I learned to recognise a couple of blue tit calls, I could tell when they were marking their territory. When a bird such as a sparrowhawk comes by, the blue tit will shout out a warning.

I was in the park on a cold winter's afternoon when I looked up and saw a blue tit. I was focused on the bird, a little chunky ball of blue, green and yellow sitting high above in a branch, making sure I wasn't going to get any closer. It was chatting away, watching all the time as I passed underneath, flipping its head left and right in the grey sky. That contact was the essence of our connection.

Even as I write this, two blue tits are calling to each other, one outside the window in the young ash tree and the other in the neighbouring garden.

Mid-May, 2020. The blue tits in the neighbour's garden are nearing their fledging period; the parents have been feeding the little fluff balls for the past two weeks. Another bird has also returned to start breeding in the UK; I recently saw and heard the swifts as they return to the town.

Over the past few weeks, the early blue tit nesters have got a head start by staying over winter and risking the early March to April weather. The rooftops are now theatres; swirling displays pass through the skyline of trees and around church spires, and their calls echo down the roads and in the parks. I can see bright blue skies full of birds opposite my flat and my attention is caught by their lively action. The blue tits have produced a successful clutch of birds for the future; they are a symbol of our own survival and perseverance.

I spent hours sat in my tent/shed bird watching at home.

North York Moors

WHEN I WAS growing up, the North York Moors were twenty minutes' drive from my home. I loved them and by the time I turned eighteen I'd realised what a gem they really are. Yes they can be bleak, but there's nowhere else on earth quite like the North York Moors National Park. My favourite times to visit are when the bluebells are flowering in spring and the heather is coming into flower in August.

This is the largest expanse of heather moorland in England and Wales, with up to 4,400 hectares of 'moo-er land'. There are 1,400 miles of public rights of way, including the Cleveland Way National Trail, which is part of England's coastal path route. Roseberry Topping sits at the top of the National Park, a treasured spear point of a beacon to the people of Middlesbrough, Redcar and Cleveland. This is a place I visited regularly with my family and my mates.

Walking from further afield towards the National Trust site, or starting at the car park below the climb, involves a short ascent through productive mixed arable and livestock fields, then around the small woodland before a steeper climb to reach the top.

The trees are still bare in mid-February, sometimes even in March. Things look sleepy as you approach and enter the wood. I have found blue tits here, shouting at me from above. As you walk along at the bottom of the climb, the long-tailed tit and green woodpecker are head turners. As the weather improves with warmer spring showers, the leaf buds swell and burst into lime-green foliage. The chiffchaff arrives, followed by the willow warbler not long after. Like many wooded areas, the ground at Roseberry is waking up with wild garlic in spring.

Towards June, the lime-green leaves rapidly turn into a thick green canopy as chlorophyll strengthens each cell. A pheasant in the long grass pokes his head out. Lambs nearby are growing in confidence; no longer stuck to their mothers' sides, they are playing more with other lambs. A blackcap trills his call and a greater spotted woodpecker chuckles through the woodland. My alert ears catch the song of a chiffchaff.

Locals enjoy the breeze on the summit, just as they did in the 1700s; the English playwright Joseph Reed mentions the local landmark in the dialogue from the 1761 farce *The Register Office*, "Lahtle Yatton aside o'Roseberry Toppin".

'Topping' is Yorkshire dialect for the Old English 'topp' of a hill. This area has fascinating names that reflect the languages that shaped the region. Old Norse words are often the origin of place names. The Norse God Odin was used for hills; in 1119, Roseberry Topping was recorded as 'Othenesberg'. The name went through various changes to become 'Ouseberry' and finally Roseberry.

Similar examples are seen in the names of settlements or farmsteads, such as Maltby and Ormesby near where I grew up; Malti was a common old Danish name, Orme was a name recorded in the Domesday Book, and 'by' means habitation. Higher up in the north-east there is Urpeth, deriving from 'ur' bison and then 'paed' for path, indicating that this was an area for wild aurochs, now extinct.

These Old Norse words merged to create the dialect used in north-east England and Yorkshire. Other examples include 'dales' meaning valleys, 'bait' as in a packed meal, 'bairn' for a young child and 'beck' for a stream.

The Topping has been a place of interest for a long time; a Bronze Age hoard was even discovered there. From the north, it looks like a hill with a jagged cliff. People often tackle it as a morning climb; at 320 metres (1,050ft) it isn't exactly high, but it offers a staggering view of the flat plain area below and the urban landscape of industrial Middlesbrough and Redcar. Further out is the North Sea coast, now a site for a large offshore wind farm.

The summit was a sugarloaf with a geological fault. The theory is that it was created after a collapse, possibly from the local ironstone or alum mining in 1902. Ironstone, jet and alum were all heavily mined in the area from the 1700s through to the Industrial Revolution.

One year at school, I completed an artwork assignment about the Topping. This was one of my favourite research projects and I spent a lot of time researching it. I climbed the hill, investigated its history and collected photos of the landscapes instead of doing maths – brilliant!

The morning sun creeps around the Topping and settles on the fields below. There is a hare in the centre of a channel cut by harvesting machinery. A mainly dry spring interspersed with brief showers leads to the arable fields being full of cereal crops.

Screeching rooks at the base of the hill call across the open land; they fill the sky with cries, calling out and responding to other, more distant rooks. This farmland is blessed with bird species that are in decline nationally. Along the field boundaries, where brown hares run and box, the lemon-yellow speck of a bird sits on the hedge and sings the song 'a little bit of bread and no cheese'. This yellowhammer is an image of our countryside heritage, if only we allow them to stay.

I used to go with my family to a well-used route at the edge of the fields where the April morning sun glistened down on the crops and the hares' ears poked through the grain stalks. Brown hares sit in their earth trenches, called 'forms'; on the right day you may catch sight of male hares chasing females. The females push, box and twist around the field, either to avoid the males or lead them onto a trail.

Hares are susceptible to illegal hunting with guns and dogs that goes on all year round. Farmers may be unaware of it as they work hard in other parts of the farm. Hunting usually takes place early morning or during the night when there are few people to witness it.

A blue-grey warm spring sky gives me the first chance

to hear the melodic song of the skylark. Look up at the sky and see this tiny bird, then feel the sun's warmth when you close your eyes. A swallow chatters; blackcaps and whitethroats call along the hedgerow from the trees across the fields.

By June, the grass has become drier and started to change to different shades of green and cream as the warm sun hits the ground. There are butterflies and flies in the rushes. The blackcap has stopped his daily call, and in his place is the sound of crickets and a song thrush.

I could not talk about this part of the National Park without mentioning Captain Cook's Monument, a sandstone hut built in memory of the explorer. He was a local lad and climbed the Topping as a bairn. If you visit, I also recommend trying the King's Head Inn just below.

Further into the national park are the sandstone cottages famed in this area along the River Dove. From anywhere in March to late April, there are bursts of flowers on the banks and field margins. Swaledale sheep wander around the village of Goathland eating the green grass. In the weeks ahead the lambs will bound less and become more skittish and wary.

You can see the street layout of the TV series *Heartbeat*. The heritage railway line is still very popular. St. Mary's Church, with its sandstone headstones in the churchyard, stands on the site of former places of worship dating back to the twelfth century. The sandstone that forms so much of this landscape can be seen on the moor tops. Inside this small church it is easy to imagine all those people who have taken part in christenings, marriages and funerals in this sacred stone enclave. The same work has been going on for centuries; there is no technology here.

In early spring, bunches of snowdrops and primrose are a common sight as white sheets of mist hover over the hard, frosted ground. Breathe now and you will see the air in front of you. Orange hawkweed, naturalised to the UK, and golden shield fern stand neat, tall and proud. The yew trees and long grass create a habitat for butterflies and dunnocks, enclosed by stone walls to keep out the nibbling sheep who roam the village freely.

The peaceful valley of Farndale offers an enjoyable river walk. The small wild daffodils are a native protected plant in the local nature reserve, which was created in 1955. A sign in the dale that has been there for years says: WARNING IT IS FORBIDDEN TO PLUCK OR INJURE THE DAFFODILS PENALTY £5.

Farmers move the lambs into nearby fields just as the daffodils emerge. They have done this for years and the sight offers a spring treat. These are two of my key annual markers. Swaledale lambs are full of life, with little black faces, big bright eyes and wee pink noses.

The local landowners, National Park authorities and walkers all contribute to conserving the habitat for the daffodils. Up to 40,000 people visit the area in a short period of time; for many of them it is often the first walk of the year and a chance to get out in the milder weather and get a 'bit of sun'.

Water flows at a steady pace, trickling over pebbles and rocks, and its sound as it moves downstream makes the place seem so tranquil. When the mist rises in the chilly

March morning air, the morning sun glimmers through the trees onto the water.

The North York Moors are the uplands and valleys of this area and Danby is a central point linking Roseberry Topping, Goathland and Farndale.

Out in the hills and dales, farms can look sleepy and lonely to the tourists driving past. Swaledale sheep, together with beef and dairy cattle, contribute a large chunk to the local economy. The Swaledale is a famous breed in North Yorkshire and the surrounding counties, and you often see them around the moor, munching and mooching along the road verges.

Together with my mate Andrew, I was fortunate enough to experience hill sheep farming throughout the year in this part of the world. Farming is hard and varied work. Financial planning for the year on the farm is key; from land type and distance from markets, right down to the amount of hay produced, are often crucial to a farm's survival.

My experiences highlighted the distance between the consumer and the farmers' view of things. More work could be done to connect the two. I would also like to see real change to the new schemes in order to enhance biodiversity. Links between the farms can stamp a mark on the area, if taken seriously.

I got very interested and invested in the work that is done in this area; it helped me understand more about life outside the cities and and supermarkets. I saw active countryside management of woodland boundaries, where woodland strips have been cared for, for over a decade. I saw the life cycle of sheep and riparian river conservation. The work was never ending.

A border collie watches his master as hundreds of ewes feed in a 'maternity ward' at a farm on the boundary of North Yorkshire.

The farmers work for themselves. They make marginal profits as each year they are affected by market prices and the weather.

One of my favourite adventures was the day my friend and I arrived to find quads, dogs and people surrounding the farm. Usually the place was silent except for the sounds of wildlife, but today was a sheep round-up day. It was one of the traditional round-ups to bring in the sheep to shear their fleeces and give them a health check during the summer.

The sheep were kept on an area of common land behind the farm, as they had been for centuries, in a traditional practice known as 'hefting'. The farmers all mark their flocks a different colour and send the sheep for part of the year to a place they are attached to because their ancestors have been kept on it for generations. The boundaries of the common land are made up of white painted stones, grouse grit trays, rivers and occasional cattle grids.

Local farmers, the sheep and their dogs are all part of an experienced team that bring the sheep in. Each collie is fit and eager, wanting to please its master – until they are not working. Then they start scrapping until someone shouts, 'Eh, pack it in!'

On round-up day, we headed for the far side of the moor top, crossing the road that leads down towards Hutton le Hole from Castleton. The sky was bright and clear and the valley on the other side looked glorious with lush green fields below and a crust of peaty brown and purple moorland above.

There were more than a hundred ewes and lambs on this side. We started to move them along and across the moor ridge to the valley below where the farm was situated. Andrew and I hopped in and out of the heather to move the sheep, then we were left at the top of the moor to look down and wait until we could see the shepherds coming from the other side, like spectators of the action below.

The farmers and dogs were magnificent. Each working dog showed its intelligence and love of work. Up high I could hear their masters' whistles, the sound of the quad engine and the sound of birds. The Swaledale sheep were moving left and right but eventually they reached the farm at the other end of the dale before the end of the hot morning. It was a job well done.

Up on the moor, the meadow pipit flitted across occasionally, the skylark was about somewhere, and the grouse poked its head up giving its 'gargle' sound.

In the late autumn, the air becomes bolder and colder. My fleece is zipped up high and I am wearing three pairs of socks; a spell of cold weather has hit before the winter comes to stay later in November.

In these valley and moor micro-climates, foliage contracts to leave a skeleton of brown heather and grasses. The hardy sheep, built for survival, are high on the moor; the cattle are tucked away in barns and you can hear the occasional low-pitched chorus as the farmer feeds the herd. Spider webs in the morning light are heavy with dew.

This is when the red grouse blend into their surroundings. I see lots of red grouse because this bird, along with the pheasant, is raised for shoots. It has a distinctive, luminous eye ring. When they congregate on the moors, they look as if they are in the middle of a meeting.

The grouse are on the boundary of the moor top, the common ground and the dry-stone walls of the lower pasture. This is somewhere I have seen stoats flit nervously in and out of the cracks of the ancient dry-stone walls. These walls are covered in lichens; orange, grey, white and brown shades, like a mini tropical forest. They are fringed with tufted grass, rushes and small trees sheltering from the elements.

Headed up Birkbrow on the winding road that leads into the National Park, past the Lockwood Beck Reservoir, looking over towards Commondale and Danby, I have seen more grouse than in any other area. The red grouse are famed in this area. Management of the moor for the benefit of one species is a controversial business with controlled burning of the heather to maintain low, fresh shoots.

I have seen loads of them on these moors at different times of the year. Often on snowy and drizzly days in the winter the grouse will be lying low, feeding on the remains of heather shoots from the earlier season. This mottled red, ginger and brown bird merges into the dried grasses and brown heather in a rugged landscape of dry-stone walls, shooting bays and moorland plateau. Just behind Roseberry Topping, my walks up to the moor provide lots of cover. If disturbed, the red grouse launches out of the heather and bilberry to find another spot nearby to hide.

The classic call of the red grouse is a gargle and it raises its head to show off its glorious bright red eyebrows.

It is classed as 'under threat' as a result of the practice

of shoots, disease and loss of rich habitats declining in quality. It would be a shame to see such an iconic and humble plump grouse species fall into decline.

A sprinkling of Red Grouse on the farm track watching from all angles

Looking across the valley at Chop Gate, North Yorkshire
National Park.

A moor top of pink heather in bloom, during August, North
Yorkshire National Park.

Reed beds

REED BEDS ARE one of my favourite places where you can see warblers, herons and dragonflies. Winding paths make you scope places and rely on sound and sight because you cannot use landscape features when you are so close to the water. Tall, thin reeds steal the view so you must peer through gaps and look to the sky if you wish to peek into the world of ancient waterways. They allow you to witness nature up close; drained and cleared by man, they have been reinstated and reclaimed by nature. The reed bed, a rhizome bed, is a system of stems. We often ignore them in favour of other things and miss the multitude of life they contain. They form a buffer between one habitat and the next. Reeds are mega growers, reaching up to two metres in height from the year that they put out shoots. This fascinates me.

In a reed bed, you follow a maze of paths created by animals, water and man. On the estuary and marshes of Hartlepool, the land is made up of flat pools, drains, flood plains and vast open, low-level wet spaces. If you are not familiar with these parts, your senses will be as heightened when you are walking alone as they would be in a woodland.

Just a few minutes' drive up the road and further into Hartlepool, Seaton Carew Road is alongside Cowpen Marsh Nature Reserve and the appropriately named Seal Sands. This estuary is part of the wider mouth of the River Tees.

Teesmouth National Nature Reserve is further up the road within this hive of industrial activity. In the past, this was one of the most polluted and damaged areas for wildlife. If you can embrace the landscape, it feels a part of urban nature.

Work to limit pollution and restore this area has been carried out over the past few decades and now waders use it for feeding and breeding. The winds coming off the sea are grim sometimes, but this wind pushes sea birds that fly along the coastline in search of food. Peregrines and short-eared owls also regularly use this area.

For many years, industry pushed away seals, though they have returned and now both Grey and Common seals use the mudflats. I spent many hours studying the wildlife in this area in every season and, from my view, if thought is given to restoration and protection, then wildlife can thrive around human activities, just like it has learnt to do in this industrial area.

-◆-

July 2016, 9am: a cup of tea from the flask with the hide window open. The ground is cool and the sun is low this morning. A female marsh harrier, with her long forward and back wing movements, is distinctive as she scans from above and swoops low, sending wader birds up into the sky. Cover is better south of the reserve, and this allows her to creep up and go unnoticed at first. Feeding teal, wigeon, mallard and lapwing are sent up into the sky, forming confused clouds as the harrier, much bigger than them, flies above. This time she is unsuccessful and watches the commotion as they fly north. She sets her sight on the next reed bed for a chance of breakfast.

In the reed pools of Teesside's Saltholme with the Transporter bridge and industry all but hidden in the distance.

The sky is blue and the sun glistens down on the pools. There are tiny movements of a stickleback in the water among the woody stems.

It is time for the conservation volunteers to get into chest-high waders and cover their faces and arms with stinky mud and sludge. They can help species thrive by controlling reed domination and ensuring there is enough water in small pools to sustain delicate species and fragile ground. Conservation volunteering can give you a natural buzz the same as any gym can. The physical work varies according to the habitat, but the results of the work give immense satisfaction.

The reeds blowing in the wind, engulfing your surroundings.

Phragmites australis, a reed species that explodes into life each spring, is a challenge. Too little work and the habitat is fragmented, too much and it dries up to enable succession. It takes a fair bit of sweat and time to make even a small dent in the large-scale areas where it flourishes. We still use small machines and tools in many reed beds, though larger modern machines can be used on bigger areas. Machines with traction over wide tyres make less impact on the land and keep the water clearer. With proper management, the banks holding the water will not fluctuate too dramatically and will retain the delicate plants and feeding areas.

The sound in a reed bed is incredible, whether it be windy or still. The typical sound of the reeds is like paper blowing or crisp, dry leaves moving on a path. The stems of the reeds are strong and rigid but have enough flexibility to sway with the wind. In a moderately small reed bed you can still get the feeling of being lost in a wilderness. Even with the noise of cars or planes nearby, you feel you are in a remote place. In the winter, you might hear the waterfowl in the distance, or the snipe flitting between the reeds and rushes.

Industry powering through the evening, as dusk brings a warm winter sunset.

The Teesside reserve is surrounded by businesses and factories. Wildlife disappeared as the area was swamped with industry and pollutants. But in this, my local reserve, it is still easy to eliminate the outside noise pollution and focus on the water rails or wigeon.

My local nature reserve rivals any forest for the range and variety of species. The sound of warblers is a useful guide to the drama of this habitat; sedge and reed warblers are just some of the birds that can be heard in the late spring and summer reed beds.

The sedge warbler uses an assortment of calls to make music, and the occasional reed warbler and reed bunting continue singing further up the spring reeds. The grasshopper warbler was sighted on the reserve one year and got a lot of attention, especially from me, as it was the first one I'd heard. Hearing a bird species for the first time is a unique experience. This small bird had travelled from West Africa to our post-industrial reserve and set up a base in a deep reed bed surrounded by thorny shrubbery.

In the spring, my favourite selection of birds arrives at the reserves. The chiffchaff sings one of the most beautiful songs. These birds have flown thousands of miles, with food stops, avoiding predators such as hawks and people who ambush them for sport and food.

In spring, shoots emerge from the water and continue to thrive as the season progresses. The summer months see the shoots and foliage reach their peak and the panorama becomes distorted by the different heights of the reeds. The ground is full of plant life, like the bird's-foot trefoil, which sparkles amongst the soil loam and dried grasses that are created with the help of cattle-trodden pathways.

We can't expect there always to be more space for our wildlife and their reed bed habitats, so it's important to maintain existing habitats. At the moment, we are still losing significant areas both locally and worldwide. Reed beds, which support precious populations, are limited in both size and number. Conservation organisations work to maintain, increase and connect the sites to make them work better for the future. Drainage work across the UK has lowered water levels and created agricultural land to replace these habitats. Now that climate change is happening and we are experiencing extreme weather conditions, drought has led to cracks in the soil and bare channels where there should be water, particularly in the east of England in parts of the Essex coastline.

The cattle egrets, little egret and great white egrets have been around in the UK for most of my life. They are less common in my home region than in the south of England. When I can, I like to spend time watching egrets and herons pop in and out of the reeds as they move from site to site.

The egrets have enjoyed colonising and expanding their range. A couple of years ago, I got to see the great white egret on Hartlepool salt marshes for the first time, and its size surprised me. How does such a large species fit into a place like this? Over time, our island has become a place of colonisation and retreat; these birds are making use of the opportunity, weaving into the landscape along with our resident grey herons. Glossy ibis may follow the same path in years to come.

There are water voles in the boundaries here, which are preyed on by the American mink. This invasive species is looking for a meal like any other animal; they could choose ducks and waterfowl, but they like a plump vole. Stable reed banks and islands allow our little vole friend to have a home. I've found their droppings (a latrine) and a feeding station, and it is easy to see why they can live here.

A long narrow clearing allows me to see into the deeper reeds and watch for shy birds coming out to feed. A grey heron emerges and stands still for about five minutes. As each minute passes, the skies change the light on his body as he concentrates on finding his next meal. The bird's yellow legs blend into the reeds; standing, watching with a beady eye and yellow bill, he is waiting for fish to swim near enough for him to pounce. This awkward, gangly bird pierces the fish successfully.

Cattle, sheep and ponies feed on different native species of plants. Some cattle trample over the ground and thicker vegetation, others fertilise it. Over time, debris increases and a fen develops, allowing more tree species and shrubs like willow and birch to become established. Litter heaps in the reed bed margins are beneficial because the excess material creates a warm place for hibernating invertebrates, amphibians and reptiles. In winter, they can keep out the colder temperatures with their slow composting. The reed bed structure can also help break down dirty water; often the roots digest material and bacteria thus cleansing the water.

Dragonflies and damselflies lurk in the water in their early stages of life until they are transformed into beautiful large-winged creatures with colours that rival any stained-glass window. The arrangement of eyes situated at the top of their head contributes to their amazing ability to become a super predator on a small scale.

In the autumn, how could you not want an experience with ducks? Migration is back on the agenda, and at my home reserve the widgeon is one species among many to move up and down the country. They may be moving to warmer climates or have come here from further north to avoid the hard ground and limited food reserves of harsher northern winters.

I studied at my home reserve in late summer and early autumn for part of my university degree. I had a fantastic chance to film at one of my favourite places and had the place almost to myself! Autumn sees a slowdown and colours begin to change to reds, browns and creams. The warm days are fewer and the weather feels a bit nippy once again.

A dabbling duck is prey, sought by carnivorous raptors, foxes and man. I sit inside the hide, keeping still and quiet so as to not alert them just twenty metres away from me.

On a dew-heavy morning, I cycle up to the hide, open the door then sit down and peer through the hatch. This morning the sun is coming up fast and in the distance I can see the plumage colours of a shoveler. In front of me are mallards. Wigeon are feeding and moving in a flock like a herd of antelope making their way across a plain.

My research was the study of behaviour in ducks, identifying species and how they observe the environment for predators. Here in my home reserve, wildlife of all sizes, including the dabbling ducks, can take advantage of plentiful cover and food. A fleeting glimpse of a duck as it moves among the reeds and in the open water allows me to see the markings of the teal, a slender bird wearing a slim suit. The male's display captivating colourful patches of chestnut brown, and their green heads are bright in the autumn sun. The females accompanying them are mottled brown but no less special to observe. The teal are just one of the fast-moving feeders out on the water and at the pool edges this morning. I sit in the hide, eating almost as fast as they do when things are calm.

The repetitive sound of the coot is disturbed with an abrupt coot call of 'tif', alerting a nearby mallard and silencing the feeding routine for about thirty seconds. The coot returns to his usual chirping after the threats have been scouted for.

The water ripples and there is the occasional plop of the ducks bobbing their heads above the water. A redshank on the muddy water's edge gives a piping, long low call followed by a short, sharper call. Dabbling ducks, swans, water rail and snipe are flitting between cover.

The more elusive bittern may be in there, extremely well camouflaged with their mottled brown and black feathers. I have only seen bittern in the air moving from one spot to another; seeing them is still a rarity in the UK and conservation work is being undertaken to provide habitats for further territories as the numbers climb once again.

＊

The winter reeds are monotone, brittle and closed off from the outside world. A beige jumper and thick, high-tog wellie socks come to mind. One species that takes me to the reed bed in the depth of winter is the humble starling. As the reed bed comes alive each evening in the winter months, there is a spectacle that is repeated across the country. Starlings from towns and the countryside come together and merge into groups in the sky called 'murmurations' before roosting; it is their version of settling down for the night. The gathering produces about fifteen minutes of brilliance as they group before dusk then roost and sleep, enjoying safety in numbers in the reeds.

One of the starling murmurations in chilly December at dusk.

Each bird following its mates to create a mass flight display and they swoop and divert to deter predators. The sparrowhawk, kestrel and peregrine falcon have a harder time picking out a single starling if they are working in the middle of the flock. The outsiders and starlings that lag behind become the predators' victims.

I have seen many predators at the roost sites, most recently a kestrel sitting on a hawthorn bush, not really interested until suddenly it picked this moment to get a meal that night. I have no idea if it was successful as the starlings continued their spectacular display until they shot down into the reeds together to roost for the evening, preserve their energy and keep warm.

Some areas have a gathering of up to 100,000 starlings, and they were reported in more than 130 locations in the first month of January 2020. An online UK map will help you find the best sites and times to see them. At one of these sites, I saw them shimmy across the skyline and fly into a nearby patch of reeds.

If you share the sight of a starling murmuration with other people, they can help pick out other groups of starlings in the distance that are moving to join the main flock. If you are alone, you'll hear the birds communicating with each other and the sound of their wings as they move in unison. Then the light fades and the murmuration blends with the grey sky until they stream into the reed bed for the night.

The RSPB reports that the starling population has fallen by more than eighty per cent in recent years.

After winter arrives, there are crisp frozen patches of ground at the water's edge amid the brittle stems. I was lucky enough to see a water rail one day with its glossy feathers standing out against the grasses, scrub and mudflats.

The waterfowl and waders continue to feed, spending most of the daylight hours feeding and resting in order to survive. The ground is frozen and air bubbles sit under the surface. As the year begins again, bird watchers refresh their yearbook, ticking off new sightings of birds.

A redshank searches for food alone in the cattle trodden pool edges at RSPB Saltholme.

Red Fox

A CONTROVERSIAL ANIMAL, the red fox is both our friend and our foe. It is a character with sharp ears and pointed features. The sleek red fox looks like a wolf put in a hot wash of red clothes and, just like the wolf, it is a victim of major resentment, as are other *Canidae* family members. In the old days the fox was the trickster, the sly thief, but in more recent decades it has won over a few people. It is, after all, fighting for survival each day just like the rest of us.

These animals adapted to their surroundings in a way that not many species have, and they've caught our attention by doing so. My mam tells me that when I was a baby they could hear the foxes in the streets. So, my first connection was made when I was very young because of my curiosity and because I didn't want to sleep.

My first memory of connecting with a red fox was hearing one call, deathly sounding shrieks just like the ones in television dramas like *Midsomer Murders*. The call is really worrying at first, and hearing it when I was a kid kept me awake, though I was not distressed. In the dark, colder months of January, the foxes called to each other with a scream. They were in the beck and fields behind my family home. The scream when they're looking for a mate is described as being like the sound of two people having an argument or, more extremely, like someone being murdered.

There are loads of videos online of the city foxes' mating calls because they have little fear of being near people. They also get replies from dogs that are furious at the disturbance. As a kid, I sat up listening and looking out of the window to catch a glimpse of a fox when the moon and stars were out, until my eyes got too heavy. Over the road there was a man living alone in a bungalow. Whenever he went away, we looked after his home. He used to feed the foxes that visited. Our neighbour worked at night and he would often see them in his garden as he left for work. I loved that idea of them being around in such secretive ways. I couldn't see them, but I was aware they were opposite our home.

Ꙫ

The gardens here connected with strips of woodland around the housing estate. My childhood home was on the former estate of a hall, which is still in the centre of all these houses. It is a plot of a few acres made up of woodland and gardens, undergoing development as I write. It is fragmented but it allows species to move between the gardens.

The idea that elusive wildlife was thriving really excited me. I would spend time watching out of the window to see if anything was around. Sometimes I explored the garden looking for signs of the foxes. Usually the trips were unproductive, though the thrill of seeing a hedgehog or a bat got me hooked.

-●

Aristotle made notes about species and helped us understand the fox. He pointed out that foxes were 'of the earth', and described them as cunning and intelligent. That is exactly right; they are not the enemy but they act intelligently to survive, avoiding people and surviving by foraging in the most efficient way they can. Unfortunately, for a very long period until the Enlightenment, the myths about foxes made them seem evil characters and that image has remained to some extent.

In rural Britain the fox is elusive, a predator to pheasants, rabbits, chickens and other ground-nesting birds such as grouse. The fox will take advantage of compost and other open bins, and pets left unaccompanied. I once caught a fox seconds before it ran off with a chicken; the chicken in its mouth was lifeless with shock before I spooked the fox by chasing after it.

It is thought of as an animal that needs its numbers managed by people through culling both in the towns and countryside. On occasion, the fox will make surplus kills. You wonder why it had to kill and cause so much damage and chaos. If the fox were just hungry, surely it would only take what it needed? It is thought that an unusual surplus of prey confuses the fox and, in its panic, it continues to kill.

The earth, the term used for a fox's den, is made by digging down around tree trunks and hedge banks. The fox earth in populated areas is different from those in natural places. Urban foxes use our sheds, decking and unoccupied gardens as temporary dens. The fox is living in most habitats and found in the majority of our bustling towns and cities; it has become adept at living in concrete jungles.

Just like many people who moved to the cities for a new life and job, some foxes have relocated to our urban areas where opportunities arose for them and even began a form of urban evolution with their success. Data shows that half the population of city foxes in London and Bristol are under a year old. They travel and hunt alone but this doesn't mean they are solitary. In urban spaces they have neighbours at every turn. If their territory includes a male and female in the same area, they scent mark to demonstrate this and show their boundaries. Regular territory markings are often in gardens, to the annoyance of some folk. Scent glands are also found on their feet.

Occasionally urban foxes cross paths and meet up physically, whereas in rural locations they might have to scent and mark across larger areas and use calls to communicate further. But in both places people view them as scavengers, hunters and hungry opportunists.

I only saw foxes in the garden once or twice, but that really stimulated my fascination with this stealthy animal. It wasn't long before I had an idea: if I played fox calls, maybe they would reply or come to investigate. What I didn't realise was that my timing was wrong; I tried it in September and October, ahead of the breeding season, and I didn't get any curious foxes or any calls back.

I tried again. To get a better chance of seeing them, I went to the front garden and played the fox calls down the road. I didn't see any foxes but I did hear a scream like the fox's – from a woman. This poor lady didn't realise I was sitting in the shadows on the garden wall.

I had a bit more luck at my nanna's garden. I was in the conservatory and a red fox poked its head up and looked around. Seeing it gave me a buzz and, just like the fox, my response was to freeze and lock eyes with it. Neither of us wanted conflict but we were startled to see each other. After a moment, the fox trotted on. It really did feel like an encounter with something from another world. It doesn't matter what animal it is, it is a buzz that I still get when I come across a creature that could bolt at any second. It is a response in the human makeup to look at them in awe, and an instinct not to disturb potential prey.

This red fox is resourceful and that is something we can respect; people are either drawn to them or repelled by their intelligence. I've read about foxes ripping the mesh from a pet rabbit's hutch, traumatising the unfortunate owner. I understand that; as a kid, I wanted the foxes to come to my garden but I didn't want them to eat my rabbits or guinea pigs. I was worried about the safety of my pets and set about deterring predators.

There were numerous tricks to deter them in the newspapers at the time, including using a device to emit high-pitched sounds. Something similar has been used to deter teenagers from hanging around outside shops! High-pitched sounds could also deter insects, rats and cats. It wasn't a method I wanted to use because I'd had a painful experience from hearing it. A noise deterrent for insects made me feel sick and hurt my ears, so I could imagine the confusion it would cause to foxes and other species.

The other tricks include a foul-scented spray or jelly, or using the urine of lions or humans. I had no way of getting hold of lion urine – but human, yes, I created a perimeter around the pets' area that the foxes wouldn't cross. My pets lived a happy long life.

-●

Fox-hunting was a popular sport in which it was said that the fox could outwit the hounds. Thankfully we are leaving that era behind, even if some people persist in it. The dogs are still bred and used for scent trails. I've seen them making ground over hillsides; something that displays human dominance over nature as the echo of the hounds' barking turns heads.

The foxhunting ban was implemented in 2005 to stop wild mammals being hunted by dogs. During centuries of hunting, some wild mammal populations were depleted and needed restocking. These hunts produced record finds; one of my favourites was the albinism, which was recorded in Northumberland in the 1940s and 1950s. Many foxes are still controlled, though not in such numbers since hunting has declined. Managed predator species have been introduced to places such as estates for game bird shoots, where chick survival is prioritised.

My next few encounters with foxes were as a teenager. The birds on the local reserve were attracting a lot of visitors, and the local fox population had decided to set up an earth next to a bird hide in full view of the public. That year I got some great views of both the vixen (the female) and the dog (the male).

With little fear, I had a companion on the route around.

From the hides I saw foxes walking at the edge of the pools and on the banks of the lakes, scattering birds into the sky and sending them into deeper water. One day when I was alone, the vixen showed herself at the hide window. I videoed her as she sneakily peered in and smelled the air. Then she gave me a look as if to say 'not another human!' and walked off the other way.

Another day in the hide I saw a vixen hunting coot chicks. Every few days she picked up another chick until they'd all been taken to feed its growing cubs. The coot had chosen a poor location to raise her brood; another year, she might have raised them successfully. The fox is opportunistic; it made perfect sense for her to place her earth near to a buffet of waterfowl. It was obvious that she wasn't bothered by people; she was aware of our presence but carried on walking over banks, disappearing and hunting.

One day I watched the dog fox in the grass. His head tilted as he focused on the sounds, and he moved his head from side to side to pick up the precise position of his next victim. This reserve is in an industrial landscape, so there was a lot of noise from factories and traffic that distracted both me and the fox; I saw his ears twitch at the wail of occasional sirens. He stood poised and then launched, his front legs curled then outstretched. It was over in twenty seconds and he was rewarded with a vole. I saw this behaviour around the site many times as I followed the foxes during different seasons. My favourite was watching him chomp down his Sunday afternoon 'scran' of a vole as he looked at the camera.

Sourcing food is tougher in the winter, and this is when the foxes latch on to eating bird seed to gain energy. That continued through the year when the vixen was hunting.

I would catch her with the cubs feasting on the seed dropped by starlings and tree sparrows. It wasn't long before I found the foxes climbing the tree. It was funny to open the hide window and see a gangly, cheeky fox staring at me at eye level from the tree, munching on suet or sunflower seeds with not a bird in sight.

This vixen's next move was to get to the seed before it was placed in the bird feeders. Some mornings, when I walked around the hides filling the feeders, the fox either joined me or she waited in the distance, watching me curiously. This fox had a reputation for getting close and she didn't want to wait any longer. I had my hands full as I poured in different varieties of seed, and I'd left a few feeders on the floor a couple of feet away. You can guess who nicked it; a gentle lifting of the tube and she ran away! Luckily, she was spooked by my panic and quick pursuit before she reached the top of the bank and she

Our ingenious red fox in the trees, startled by me opening the hide.

dropped the feeder. This was one of the last times I saw her before the end of her family's reign over the reserve. This generation had taken advantage of the reserve's abundance of waterfowl and bird seed; it is an indication of their brilliant level of intelligence and craft.

That particular year the cubs grew up and started looking for new territories, venturing off the reserve and risking their lives. I saw at least one killed on the road and by the end of the year the remaining foxes had dispersed or fallen victim to traffic. Animals like the fox cubs are not fearful and they have no experience of roads. Small animals don't always cross successfully. I saw a roadkill badger and two hedgehogs a couple of weeks ago. This is a theme across the globe. In South American countries they see numbers of giant anteaters killed on the highways, and in Australia the red kangaroo and emu fall foul of them too.

Bridges and underpasses act as nature's bridges, and we know that animals use them more and more when given the chance to adapt to our changes. These will hopefully be used more in the designs of roads, to prevent wildlife being hit by cars.

At university in Cumbria I saw the secretive side of the rural fox. They turned out to be much, much harder to find! I used hair samples to learn about them and looked for evidence of where they were but I couldn't find them. One day, when I was expecting to see a ginger-haired fox in the small town of Ambleside, it turned out to be a badger! It was a long time before I even heard a fox. Part of the problem was the presence of a pack of hounds on the edge of the fell. Hundreds of years of being hunted have affected the foxes' responses to the low barks and scent of the hounds. It was clear that the foxes actively avoided people and dogs in this area where tourists flock during the day. At night, when it is quiet, dark and cool, it is their time.

When I was studying mammal populations with remote camera traps, I didn't see one in the small study area of the Lake District National Park I was working in. Then my friends and I went to Blackpool one day and I saw an urban fox within a few hours, where it took me weeks to find one on evening walks in the National Park.

◆

Scavenging foxes couldn't stay in brick streets and alleys and they didn't have parks and larger gardens to explore until the late nineteenth century. It was the post-war housing boom and the development of a suburban boundary, with its gardens and open spaces, which introduced the fox and a wide range of other animals to what is on offer in present day towns. Shrubbery, trees and small rubbish bins offered shelter and food and were ideal locations to raise a family. Rail tracks gave them the opportunity to move from one area to another, and that keeps the flow of genes healthy.

For the first half of the twentieth century, foxes were

reported to be living fearlessly amongst people in London and Bristol, and were seen most frequently at dawn and dusk. Their ability to adapt to different situations has successfully revived their numbers in parts of the country where they were hunted out. Now you can see foxes everywhere, and they have a surplus of waste food and prey in the towns.

So, why do we actively feed foxes? Perhaps it is because we like to see and feed animals of many kinds; some people love feeding birds in their garden, and others will get pleasure from seeing a fox enjoying a piece of chicken that has been offered.

Foxes are one of our many neighbours and they deserve respect, but feed them with caution. You wouldn't like your neighbour to stop them coming back. The press has given the fox a hard time but they don't show the side of which I am aware, of an animal trying to survive in the modern world we have created in urban and rural areas.

I've seen some great photos of urban foxes against backgrounds of city street lights but the two photos of red foxes that caught my eye are in very different situations. The first was taken by Don Gutoski and shows a white, snowy image of the Arctic Circle where the wind and temperature can clearly be seen to affect the red fox's struggle for survival. A stunning ginger-red fox holds the bloody, lifeless body of the smaller Arctic fox in its mouth. The image captures the scale of each fox and shows how the red fox has moved further north, encroaching on Arctic fox territories. The red fox can adapt to changing climates and landscapes; if it crosses paths with different subspecies, it can dominate them. This may happen with other species as climate change removes the barriers between environments, and new species gain a foothold in areas that previously were the reserve of specialist species.

In the second photo I admire, Adrian Bliss captured a room of crumbling blue walls and a wintry scene of snow outside the window in Pripyat in the Ukraine. Dormant trees and buildings reflect the cold. In front stands a stunning red fox, as alert as ever. The last thing you notice is the litter of gas masks surrounding the animal. One mask hangs from a wooden chair behind the fox. The image is haunting, showing the animal as a beam of life in a carpet of man's devastation and destruction.

Deer

BRITAIN'S TWO FULLY indigenous deer are the red and the roe. These two species received the Forest Law of William I (1087), which gave them legal protection to only be hunted by the king. Britain's largest living land mammal is the red deer – a very majestic animal – and that's the one you see in images of the Scottish mountains (Munros).

In the north-east of England there are no indigenous wild red deer; the remaining indigenous populations are in the south-west of England and in Scotland. In times gone by, deer were prey upon by man and victims of habitat change. The date of their extinction is not known in Northumberland; in Durham, as few as forty or fifty deer were recorded after a harsh winter snowfall around 1673.

There is something medieval or ancient about a stag, whether it's his stature, his hide or antlers. We tend to forget their large size; in our modern towns and villages the largest thing to run around would be a domesticated horse.

My first chance to understand red deer came via the television when I was growing up. I watched a BBC series that showed them rutting in the autumn when they gather for this spectacular mating season. I was fascinated; where were they, where could I see them? The ones on TV were on the Isle of Rhum, and I wasn't likely to see any in the north-east of England where they have been expelled from their habitats and driven to extinction.

My first chance to see red deer was at Studley Royal Deer Park at Fountain's Abbey, a National Trust site. I first went in the summer to watch how the deer behave; here they feel safe and this gave me a chance to watch herds for the first time, feeding and moving across the parkland. This park has ancient large trees and stone-wall boundaries as well as good grazing.

I had to work out the differences between sika deer and red deer. The two have been together in the wilds of the UK for years now as sika deer is an introduced species from Asia. Breeding can occur between them. Sika deer are smaller in size, with a smaller head and spots on the females.

I visited the same site in the autumn season in October. The grass was still vibrant green, though the trees had started their transition to oranges, reds and browns before the leaves went crisp and fell. The rustling of a million crisp leaves in the breeze reminds you that harder times are about to come and that the season is changing. In the park, the tree line holds a very strong horizontal line, just above the reach of the deer.

The stag deer in the park consist of strong males, each

with a harem of females that stick together and feed on the pasture and occasionally are rounded up or followed by the male. The idea of 'stag dos' before a wedding goes back to celebrations by military comrades; the term doesn't refer to the stag deer but to males in general who are strong and healthy, in the prime of their lives.

I'd watched videos as research, so I knew what to look for to see rutting behaviour. Animals in the *Cervidae* family (including deer, moose and elk) grow antlers. Changes in their hormones allow for growth of these bony structures covered in velvet, which harden up, ready for this moment.

One morning, I saw the red deer stag trot down the track out of sight with its head high. The sound of its roar could be heard across the pasture, echoing on the bare, cold ground and against the trees, which absorbed the sound. The ornamental delicate red and orange trees were buffered by tufts of green and cream grass and rushes. This set the scene in an ancient parkland landscape, hundreds of years old, where the majestic royal beast roams in all its glory. I could see that some hinds had left the main herd whilst the other herd members continued to eat. The stag crossed the road to join the herd, and the current stag protecting his patch picked up his head. This was just what I was waiting to see.

Males compete for mating rights. Within a few seconds the two stags started to jog over to each other; it didn't look intimidating, it was just a burst of energy. Once they were about five metres apart, their body language changed. It was very quiet and I had expected more noise, but suddenly they locked antlers with incredible force and the primal sound of antlers clashing echoed around the open space.

These two stags tussled for a few seconds as my family and I watched with delight. Before they separated, the stags had worked out who was stronger. One stag unlatched and ran away quickly as the other stag chased him out of his patch and away from his harem. Full of testosterone and power, the stronger stag roared at the other male to display what he had achieved. Not only had I seen this, I had a recording of the action on a camcorder too. It captures my best experience of rutting stags tussling for hinds in the deer park. I have the film still.

During rutting, stags stop feeding to prioritise defending their territory and mating with the hinds. They rest where and when they can, even if it's only for five minutes. Some of the older and weaker stags don't get through the winter because of exhaustion.

Stags showing off their power and testing each other in battle at Studley Royal deer park.

It can take up to three weeks for the stags to serve (mate), during which they must guard their patch to hold the herd together. This gives them time to pass on their genes before they are pushed from the top of the tree (or grass in this case) by younger, stronger stags.

The roar of a stag, the call of the monarch of the glen, is impressive. Female red deer have been found to have a preference for stags with deeper roars; this is also seen in fallow deer species where the larynx (voice box) drags downwards. The stag's roar is useful for sizing up the opposition without locking antlers against lesser stags, thus preserving energy and helping with their survival.

❧

The open parkland had few sounds of nature on this damp morning. Passing cars and conversation dominated the area. Then a robin took the stage and sang a beautiful song, followed by the call of a single jackdaw. This one was very vocal and soon a large group of jackdaws were circling the ancient trees and flying across to perch on a tree next to St Mary's church.

The following year, I went back to see the deer in the summer when they'd been through the winter. The chances of seeing a newborn were slim; during the first few days of life the calves are hidden and building their strength. The mother goes off to feed, leaving them during the day, only returning to feed them milk later. This limits predators from knowing where the young animals are located. In the past these predators were wolves and bears; now they are foxes, eagles and man.

❧

Red deer were probably larger in size in the past, evidenced by skulls that have been found from thousands of years ago. Deforestation, reduction in food and possibly hunting affected this. At Moking Cave in Teesdale there is evidence of larger deer and, incredibly, the bones of brown bear, lynx and wolf. Deliberate extermination of the wolf in the medieval period was carried out to protect deer for hunting by the privileged classes.

Kirkdale Cave in North Yorkshire held bones of prehistoric animals that once lived in my area, including hippopotamus, giant Irish elk and cave hyena. I was always mesmerised by the Irish elk because of its sheer size. The size of the antlers was remarkable, up to 3.6 metres wide. This is the fauna of a time long gone, though man would have encountered these thousands of years ago; only animals capable of surviving in the changing British Isles remain.

One autumn, we visited Exmoor National Park as a family so I could explore and find stags with the help of the one and only Johnny Kingdom. We explored the moorland and valleys, which resemble the North Yorkshire National Park in landscaping and management. There are fewer sheep and more large herbivores such as red deer and Exmoor ponies. I had a fantastic time in this part of the world with a great guide to show us how and where to find the wild Exmoor red deer herds in the rutting season. Our best views were of a stag who was taking a five-minute kip, obviously knackered from all the work during the mating season so far.

	Red deer	Roe deer
Breeding season	September to November	July to September
Males	Stag	Buck
Females	Hind	Doe
Young	Calf	Fawn

The history of roe deer is just as interesting. In 1338, the Court of Kings changed roe deer to fair-game status, which could have played a big role in their extirpation. By the 1800s, they were reported extinct in England and Wales; however, evidence shows that could be wrong, even with reintroductions to southern England. The Hexham area reported deer in the early 1700s, and in Cumberland and Northumberland, John Millais stated a few remained in 1906. By 1970, when Kielder Forest had been established for more than forty years, the rangers who managed the deer population stated that 1,200 roe deer were being culled each year to limit tree damage. The populations were growing further.

Roe deer lived near my home; growing up, I saw them quite often. My family and I would go through the underpass to the woodland on the hunt for deer. I would ask them to wake up in the dark on the coldest winter mornings to get a head start on the dog walkers and runners. This was the best time to see the deer and the lack of people meant we could scope the area undisturbed. The roe deer blend in so well to the wintry drab and dormant woodland landscapes.

When the sun started to rise, the grey squirrel poked out from a sycamore tree. It was joined by the wren and robin starting their winter dawn chorus. The sun wove through the sycamore, blackthorn, ash and oak – and then we saw a roe deer's white rump, just the sign we were looking for.

This was when I gained skills in stalking animals to get a better view of them. This meant following tracks, looking at formed earth where deer have bedded down to rest only a few hours previously and, importantly for me, avoiding other people. I had become more connected to the environment.

This place was close to my school and I explored it as much as I could. Some days after school I would go home this way just to see what was about and nearly always arrived home with my uniform covered in mud.

There is something very primal about being in the wood with prey animals that are listening and watching in order to avoid us. You have to be silent, watch your footsteps and breathe quietly. We saw a lot of deer for a few years in the wintertime when the fields were bare. In the summertime it becomes much harder to spot them as there is more cover and more variety in their diet, so encounters are less frequent and more random. The growth in the foliage makes it harder to spot them, and early morning sun before 5am gives them chance to feed for longer without us being around.

In the next few years, I saw something change: the

disturbance to the country park felt like it increased. Accidentally – and on purpose – people were affecting the quality of the wood. The worst point was when plans were put forward to build 400 homes on the greenfield site beside the country park. As the demand for housing increases, greenfield sites are being eaten up. A statement said: 'the park will benefit from 2,000 to 100,000 people using it'. However, increased use will further impact on the woodland's biodiversity and fragmentation of habitat. Those homes have not been built yet, but I imagine they will appear in time.

January 2018, 8am

Several spiders' webs hang over the grass and a wood pigeon calls that his 'toe is bleeding', followed by the familiar jackdaw 'jack'. Sunday morning is quiet, especially on the edge of Ambleside in term time. Nook Lane, a track up to the fells, is where I took my photograph of the roe deer. They were as surprised as I was that we came across each other.

The deer tiptoed across the damp, claggy, leaf litter and slowly walked away once it realised that I was watching. The scent of the countryside in the early morning is one of dew on the grass. At the edge of wet woodland, you can pick up an earthy, decaying smell. Bramble strangles the edge of a field making a natural barbed fence for the roe deer to hide behind and feed. This was one of many encounters as I started to map the routes taken by the deer around this edge of Ambleside. Maybe generations of deer have lived quietly in the private woods and boundaries to this area, clinging onto their range just long enough to recover their population.

Tracking the Roe dee in Cumbria.

House Sparrow

A VERY CHATTY bird, the house sparrow often gives a big talk to the community. They really are a street gang, standing on street corners and in gutters. Hedges go silent for a few seconds as you pass by, then they carry on their conversation in full voice. Sadly, not everyone can relate to my experiences of the house sparrow; their numbers have been declining since the 1970s at least.

When you step outside your house, the chances are you will get a sudden rush of sounds and sensation. The outside environment affects our senses when we leave our comfortable houses. My first thought is to look around to observe nature.

Imagine a tiny young sparrow sitting at the edge of a hedge. In the summer months they have chicks fledging everywhere; it is a frenzy of life on the estate for the sparrows. On average they can live up to four or five years, giving them ample opportunity to pass their genes on and grow the local community, if only they can survive and thrive.

The house sparrows are some of the most communal birds we have but suddenly they began to vanish. Why?

We can only presume that increased use of chemicals (such as pollutants from cars) has decimated their insect supply, together with disease and removal of their nest sites. The real reason for the decline has not been found yet and research continues.

Denis Summers-Smith, one of the world's leading experts on sparrows, lives not far away from me. His reviews suggest a decline as early as the 1920s when there was less available nesting material (straw, hay, horsehair and manure from horses) as horse-drawn vehicles were replaced by motor vehicles. Once the lack of nesting reaches a certain level, it may lead to poor reproduction levels. The 'chirp, chirp' from the hedges or the gutters is still here, but it is less than before. The sparrow has 10,000 years of connection to humanity but now we've tipped them, like many species, over the edge.

One of the earliest bits of research I did as a kid was to make grid square surveys to assess the squashed flies on cars and number plates. Science shows that fewer flies are round today, up to 50% less than 2004, but isn't that good? Unfortunately not, our family car used to have flies all over the number plate when we went into the countryside but now I don't see many at all when I do the same routes fifteen years later. This is a worry for a large variety of wildlife and can have a dramatic effect on those that need small insects in order to feed successfully and reproduce.

The sparrows share their behaviour freely in a performance right in front of us. They shout to each other, push each other around, dive to avoid predators, and shout when food is available. We are lucky to get a chance to experience such a social bird; these little fluff balls are not timid or quiet around us like some species. They are the cheeky chap on the corner.

Over the field and beck from our house was the old Spencer Beck farm where the house sparrows lived. They never ventured into the gardens but stayed local to their area and lived where food was available. They were helped by the long grass and trees, and the horses that were kept in the fields.

In 1960, a report was made of a house sparrow taking a thrown-away cigarette to its nest as material on a thatched roof and setting fire to a house in Saxmundham. That's a good reason not to smoke!

I connected more with the sparrow's way of life when we moved to a new house, where the garden was blessed with hedges and privacy. With everything I had heard about their declining numbers, I was sure they needed a reserve and I wanted to help my sparrows to flourish and repopulate the area. I even planned to puncture a hole in a corner of the roof felt in the loft to give the sparrows a warm space to shelter and nest in spring. It was a bad idea; I think my parents would have found out when a leak came through the ceiling. I decided not to and spent my money instead on a communal nest box.

Next, I decided to make a feeding station for them and other birds. The right location was key to getting the sparrows to stay and give me a chance to study and record them. It worked: they flocked in for food every day of the year, along with the dunnocks, pigeons and – once – a canary. It isn't very Mediterranean in Middlesbrough, but I guess the bird had managed to get out from somewhere and it brightened up our garden for a while.

I bought some extra hedging to create a natural background screen and set up my hide (the garden shed) to have the feeding station and perch branches in position for the cameras.

I built a nest box in my bird hide with CCTV, and a hedgehog house next to it with a camera in it as well. I had the best time setting these up and getting on with things I wanted to create; it was a perfect occupation for a teenager who avoided other people. I had the best set-up in the housing estate. The bird hide was a huge success; I had an amazing view of the birds and the sparrows had a base and our support. My mam, dad and I put out kilos of seed each month.

Occasionally, I saw the tail end of a sparrowhawk as he swooped into the area and hid behind the shelter belt I'd made. One afternoon a female sparrowhawk sat on the fence. This was the start of my relationship with sparrowhawks and my first chance to discover what they were all about. Had it known I was there, it would have shot off over the fence.

Mr and Mrs Sparrowhawk were comfortable in the garden and they liked to watch the sparrow community, which was probably a bit off putting for the sparrows! The male sparrowhawk became a regular in our garden.

This species is a top predator with many hunts being successful. As its name suggests, the sparrowhawk does kill sparrows but will also hunt pigeons, blackbirds and other small birds. It would grasp these poor sparrows in the air or on the ground and take them to a post in our fence for a swift but gruesome kill. Usually the shock was enough to kill the little sparrows. The sparrowhawk's large yellow eyes scope around after a kill, aware that at any minute another predator could steal its food.

After a while, the sparrows' calls were something I could connect with each day, from the moment the sun rose in the morning to its final rays in the evening. I can hear a sparrow chatting now down the street from my flat. Even if they're in another garden nearby, you can still hear them. Their chirp and rustle in the bushes is reassuring, as if you have someone with you. I don't enjoy walking somewhere silent.

My local area at Normanby has a car park with a boundary of low bushes, shrubs and plants, with a few trees. This is a canny little place to walk around when there isn't any traffic. You can see dunnocks, blackbirds, wood pigeons, collared doves, fieldfares and house sparrows. When the council decided to cut back the shrubs, they didn't leave them at a decent height where the sparrows could thrive, instead it was at a pitiful low level. Unfortunately in many places, biodiversity is lost and not replaced. People cut their grass and forget that species of grasses and clover won't go to seed or flower; each cut of the grass lowers the diversity of plant species. The decline of house sparrows has been noticed on the

RSPB Big Garden Birdwatch. And if that wasn't bad enough, their decline has been linked to avian malaria.

❦

I pulled up to a traditional farm on the North Yorkshire Moors. As I slammed my car door shut, I set the farm dog barking in the yard. I made out a border collie watching from the other side of the barn door.

Away from the barking dog, the breeze took away the silence and I heard a meadow pipit call and a ewe start bleating. As I headed over to the restless collie to calm her down, I could see and hear the community of sparrows watching me from the gutters and corners of the old dairy. It wasn't long before the house sparrows went back into full conversation as they had been doing before I arrived. The old stone barns were full of crevices and openings that offered refuge from birds of prey, rats and cats. Even the modern steel and Yorkshire board buildings next to the farmhouse were a good place to hang around, providing bright and airy spaces to nest and roost in.

The little sparrows hopped around the roof of an old David Brown tractor, in and out of the hay and straw stacked up in the barn. This farm has evolved over the years; the types of animals in the yard have changed and now the barns are vital holding spaces for sparrows to exploit. The house sparrow, *passer domesticus*, has found sanctuary in agriculture over millennia. Spilt seed, flies from animal faeces and plenty of sites to shelter in and move between, have allowed them to thrive amongst farmers and country folk.

—

There is a story about a Chinese leader who decided to remove sparrows to stop them stealing crops and damaging food production in the fields. They were seen as a pest. People set about killing sparrows but forgot that they eat huge volumes of insects during their breeding season when the crops are growing. Crop production actually reduced after the removal of the sparrows, as there were more opportunities for insect life to munch through the crops. Locust numbers increased and ate vast areas of crops, resulting in famine. This is a warning that wildlife mismanagement and ecological disasters are tied together.

—

I see the house sparrows as the eyes of the street; they're always out and about and busy. Creating a sparrow street is an activity encouraged by the RSPB to help sustain healthy breeding populations. My own terrace box was used by blue tits for the first two years! Finally, the sparrows moved in and raised their families in my box. I hope my work played a part in the success of the sparrows on the estate. It gave me a chance to enjoy watching the bird community and explore their lives.

The last decade of research has shown that the declining

numbers of sparrows may be stabilising and they are venturing back to places they haven't been in for many years. In London, the site around London Zoo acted like a refuge; hopefully they might eventually spread further. Perhaps more investment in their and other species recovery will be granted so that more people can appreciate the connection between man and species like the house sparrow, *passer domesticus,* something that has been a part of 'belonging to the house' for many centuries.

Lake District

THE LANDSCAPE AND community culture are treasured in this part of the world. Tourists come and go, but each night they retreat, leaving the skeleton of the place and the true life in this pastoral landscape. The slate roofs of the white-painted houses are covered with spongy green moss. Tall windows draw in light and give the bonus of great views of the towns and mountains. Each house has its centuries-old connection to the landscape. Some have dry-stone walls around their gardens and beyond, and each of these walls contains an incredible ecosystem with many species of lichens, moss, fern, grass, beetles, pipits, rabbits and stoats. From one generation to the next, the skills have been passed on to build these walls and maintain this landscape.

I am fascinated by the connection between the fells, water and the people. Ice-Age glaciers have created the U-shaped valleys with their craggy tops, and the landscape has been carved to form fells of peat, stone and rock. Ten of the current fifteen national parks in the UK include upland areas. Here we preserve features that could be overwhelmed by our need for tidiness and manicured places. The Lake District National Park is one of the latest sites to be given UNESCO National Heritage status.

I was lucky enough to visit this area each year with my family and that gave me an understanding and connection with it from an early age. I spent my university days living here in a place that kept me level during my late teens, acting as a safe and sound place that allowed me to thrive. I learnt a lot, though I had to spend more time at my desk than other students in order to keep up because academic work has never been my strong point.

Whilst at university I used every opportunity to explore. My mates and I spent a lot of time on the Keswick to Lancaster bus route, using our bus passes to full advantage on the 555.

I usually start my year in January when things start to pick up. However, I saw heading to university as a new adventure and a new 'year', albeit one that started in September.

The weather played a significant part in my time there. In my first few weeks at university it was like any typical late summer with bright, warm, sunny days before moving into classic autumnal changes. In September, the young swallows are left by their parents who start their own journey back to Africa to spend the winter in a warmer climate. The young swallows are less talkative than their parents but just as mobile in the air, giving demonstrations in the early morning as the sun burns off the dew and mist. These swallows are testing their ability and start to group together before they join the rest of the adults heading south in their first big migration. When they've gone, the skies suddenly feel empty for a short period before migrating birds like fieldfare and geese start to move down from Scandinavia.

One year, while I was living in the village, we had a bumper year of berries in the hedgerow at our doorstep. It grew on the skeleton of a crumbling wall and was topped with glossy, barbed bramble bushes. The warmth from the walls keeps the hedges full of butterflies, and flies were buzzing among the green and purple fruit. My friend Tom and I walked back from picking blackberries one day, snaking through the village back to the house, trying to hide our hands which were stained black and purple – it looked like we were covered in blood.

During my first year living in the North West, I travelled into the National Park by bus. Most days were similar: lots of tired freshers who'd stayed up late making the hour-long journey then arriving in a downpour. The wind was strong on the hillsides but much less lower down than the east-coast wind I was used to. This part of the Lakes is sheltered by the western fells so what it lacks in wind it makes up for in rain; in the colder months, rain showers are common most days.

The bus journey gave me time to sit and watch the world around me as the landscape changed from the Arndale Area of Outstanding Natural Beauty to the first hills of the National Park. You can see Reston Scar from the A591. The fields on each side are dappled with sheep in dry-stone enclosures; primitive boxes built the same way they have been for many generations.

Rainfall regularly tops up the bodies of water, and the veins of the area are the becks, ghylls, rivers and streams. The brilliance of the fell, the sheer rawness of blank hillsides, rocks, water-filled bogs and ancient stone walls are something to admire. The name Lake District is a bit of a misnomer; there are sixteen bodies of water but only one, Bassenthwaite, is a lake. The rest of them are waters, meres and tarns.

This period flips from warm late summer to indications of the winter ahead. In the first winter, I looked for the first snowfall on the hilltops. I liked coming into the village and seeing what had changed over the past few days. Had the river level increased? Was the heron there? What about the dipper? What was in the window of The Apple Pie shop? Each weekday in term time, a gaggle of students (some with suitable clothing and some not) walked the grounds and gardens of the campus. I had my trusty raincoat and walking boots. Wainwright's advice should not be overlooked: 'There's no such thing as bad weather, only unsuitable clothing.'

As I've said, rain is an ever-present feature in this region. Borrowdale was named the wettest inhabited place in England in 2009 after 300mm of rain fell in 24 hours. Tourists on wet days – and I've been one of them – seek out gift shops and cafés, which makes for thriving businesses in the area.

A winter in Cumbria is beautiful. Walking at night under the stars with the streets empty of tourists is the best part of the day. The cold gets to your ears, nose and toes. You look up and can make out the boundaries of the valley with the large fells and crag tops solid black against the wallpaper of stars. As you walk past each home, you can smell wood burning from the chimney. Returning from a walk in the dark usually woke the nearby sheep that were resting down the fields; once, I saw a common toad make a dash across an empty road.

Dark, damp mornings and evenings blend into one in the depth of winter. Waterproofs hang continually from curtain poles and door frames to dry off. My hats are lined up next to my socks, prepared for the drizzly rain the next morning.

In the winter, Herdwick sheep come into their own as a typical, hardy, coarse wool breed. Thick boned and surviving tough winters, there is still a market for their wool, though it has diminished. One year on my birthday, the blizzards overcame the view and the visibility was non-existent; for a brief ten minutes it can be scary to be caught out like this. I couldn't even see my friends who were only metres ahead, and we had to sit and wait, luckily it wasn't too long. We kept talking to one another and eventually, after we'd eaten, we carried on as the storm departed for the next hilltop. It wasn't something we expected from the forecast but I'm grateful we hadn't suffered too greatly on that hillside. The weather in this climate is truly wild.

I found the lack of tourists in the mid-term seasons made the area slow and sleepy, but the character of the local people and nature endure, waiting for the next burst of life. What an opportunity to play some football under the views of the horseshoe from Red Screes and Fairfield

Pike. Ambleside United FC's pitch had been soaked, so the park pitch was set up. It became a favourite of ours, although it was a mud bath when it had been pouring down all week. It was good fun sliding into tackles and sinking all over the place, though not so much fun for the groundsman, who gave us a shout one day, 'Give it a rest lads!'

They say that the Lake District is beautiful because it rains, but in 2009 the media was full of the terrible news of flooding and strong winds. Unfortunately this has happened more recently too; just a few months back in 2020, people across the UK and Ireland suffered from 'Storm Ciara'. Homes flooded in Appleby, the river Kent overflowed in Kendal, a landslide stopped the West Coast rail line, and the Great North Air Ambulance was put out of action by flooding at its Cumbria site. Such devastation keeps happening and each time it feels worse than the last. Is there a pattern of flooding and other weather events getting worse? Of course.

I witnessed 'Storm Desmond' in the winter of 2015 and documented the dramatic weather. Research on the sediments in Bassenthwaite Lake showed that it caused the biggest flood in more than 500 years.

Earlier in the autumn, before the storm arrived, my bedroom was positioned to make the most of the beautiful view. My desk overlooked the houses, trees and the stream on the other side of a grassed area. This stream was usually a gentle trickle. Higher up, closer to the fell top, we'd found a waterfall and pool surrounded by private woods, ideal for swimming in, despite the water being freezing. The waterfall was a strong force at the time and the water coursed from it down to the edge of town and eventually into Windermere.

Where I lived, there were the usual downpours but the river levels were still low. The studying and my job were keeping me busy but I remember seeing a weather forecast for a very wet weekend ahead.

The rain pelted down and hadn't stopped by the afternoon of the Saturday 4th December 2015. I could see it gushing down the concrete drain on the housing estate. Looking up the hill, water was flowing through the lower dry-stone walls off the fields above. At that point I started to wonder how bad it would be for us. Our house was in a fortunate position where water would flow around it and down to the lower levels. Our neighbour had her head out of the window and was cussing at the flow across her garden off the hillside and onto the road. We couldn't help her; we didn't have anything for flood defences.

The Environmental Agency came to have a look during this heavy period of rain. The bottom of the housing estate was connected to Rydal Road, which was pooled with flooding water. Tom and I went to see some friends who were in a bottom-floor flat on Rydal Road. The water was now two steps away from the level of their flat (luckily it didn't get in because of sandbags). I went in and found one of them half asleep on the sofa, not aware of what was going on!

We went to see the rest of the village. The river was twice its normal depth and the size and the volume of water coming into it was incredible; it was crashing and lashing down where a small river had been days beforehand. As you looked up to the fells you could see streams coming off the fell, not flowing down gently but dropping straight onto the fields, turning patches of them into brown and rocky splattered soup.

For a while, the main road to Waterhead after the Log House Restaurant was accessible only by all-terrain vehicles. We walked into Waterhead and saw the water creeping up to the pub on the shore. The frail jetties and the boats moored there were struggling with the height of the water. Unsurprisingly, the mute swans were not their normal macho selves in the choppy water. The few swans and ducks we saw were bobbing up and down and around. Two cormorants flew in the distance very close to the surface, their streamlined bodies gliding at speed.

As we walked back, we saw the progress of the water at the Stock Ghyll. This is generally a peaceful waterfall in the centre of Ambleside, usually framed by a green carpet of vegetation and mosses on the rocks. This day, brown water was churning and thundering down into and straight out of the village.

Further north, the A597 to Keswick was closed because of a landslide that had caused part of the road to collapse. Between the 4th and 5th December 2015, 405mm of rain fell at Thirlmere. Homes in Carlisle, Keswick, Ambleside, Kendal and Lancaster were flooded and without power. I was witnessing the damage all around us; even more was discovered once the storm had passed.

The impact assessment by Cumbria County Council states: 'the damage adjacent to the rivers, damage to the peat bunds, loss of bog areas and upland planting removed on the commons. Debris was washed onto meadows, potentially damaging fragile habitats … overall estimated at around £7million.'

The aftermath saw my favourite route for running suspended; Millers Bridge was closed until March for assessment and repair. The river, like many across the district, had churned stone and rocks into the fields and park, littering them with fencing, wood and rock. I went to a hill sheep farm and part of the work there included tidying up the shale, stone and fencing spread over the field in the aftermath of the storm. Trees had fallen, slates disappeared, stones were everywhere, and field gates had acted as sieves for branches, stock fencing and leaves.

Later that year, people started adapting their homes if they had not previously done so and could afford to. I saw one of the holiday homes where the ground floor had been changed so that sockets and other features were higher up the walls. Stone flooring, windows and door barriers were installed in some houses. One house at the bottom of our road was sadly empty for a lot longer than most; it was a cottage and it took a long time to make it habitable again. I was really pleased to see the lights on later in the year.

As late as May 2016, Keswick was still studded with sandbags. Things had moved on and my favourite escape over Millers Bridge had been repaired, allowing me to get out running and walking over that side of the valley. Storm Desmond caused destruction and it won't be the last one to impact the area; unfortunately, storms have affected areas again in 2020. More needs to be done to make their impact less devastating, using both artificial and many more natural means.

The river settled again. Rivers and dippers are a perfect combination, and the dippers return to protect their patch and raise young each year. Their white bellies and light-brown plumage camouflage them in the riverbank habitats – their bellies blend with the light sky when they're in the water searching for prey. The year before the storm, I'd watched a family of dippers back on the same stretch of river raising a family. The calls of the dipper through the trickling of the water continue; life does move on when it is given chance to recover.

Rugged Herdwick sheep watching walkers with Wastwater, England's deepest lake, nestled beneath Wasdale,

Spring

From Scafell Pike, England's highest point, you can see Scotland, Ireland and Wales on a clear day – but the chances are you won't get a decent enough day. I haven't been up when it is sunny and the weather is rarely on your side! You don't have to climb all the way to the top to connect with the landscape. Being on the wild fells, or any hill in the uplands, makes you feel you have accomplished something. For many people, just getting out is a good enough achievement. Looking at the landscape with its sharp, rocky features includes you in the environment as soon as you step out of the car or bus. The views change as you get higher. Imagine looking across the fells of Yewbarrow, Wastwater, Green Gable and Great Gable, their sheer scale and the winding streams and green fields dotted with trees in the valleys below. With every few metres of height that you gain, you experience a different view.

My first walk up Scafell, led by other university students on outdoor courses, allowed them to test their navigation skills... we ended up going to the wrong destination. It was too tiring and wet to turn back, so we decided to finish on Great Gable but at least that meant we'd conquered another peak. The green, flourishing landscape in the valleys below provides food and shelter for birds and animals. When you are high up above the top of the trees surrounded by bare, harsh, cold mountain, you know your place.

·

One of my favourite shots of Langdale on a crisp autumn day.

I was lucky enough to see Coniston water lit up by a dusk summer sun.

Swifts move into the Lake District around May. Hawkshead is great for flying around: it has wet fields and wide spaces all around, with old stone houses to nest on. The swifts converge around the village and nest on local houses. Their speed, and the amount of time they can spend in the air, is incredible for a little bird. They can leave the nest and not rest again for up to two years. Swallows and house martins also zip across the fields and wet pastures looking for food around the horse and sheep dung and the flowers. They make a lot less noise than the swifts as they flit around looking for nesting places in overhanging roofs just as the tourists begin to fill the village once again.

-●

I'd watched television pieces about Joss Naylor and often seen his books in shop windows of the Lake District. I wanted to try a Fell run, although I knew I couldn't do a full one. I didn't enjoy it.

I can do runs on level and low gradients and I'd found a familiar route involving a mixture of road, pathways and fields. It was often so wet I'd sink and slip about. I followed the River Rothay, going straight out of the house, down into town and along the public footpath towards and around Rydal Water. The route was an escape from my studies and the lifestyle I was getting used to. The challenge of the outdoors began to kick in. Putting on walking shoes, knowing that only a few metres away was a place I could be alone and use my senses, gave me an appreciation of time away from a phone and people. I needed that burst of life after a day in front of the screen cooped up in a flat or student house. My excuse was I needed to stay healthy but I couldn't wait to get outside. What better way than running into the countryside, in the quiet of the evening in the Lake District? The only other people about were tired hikers, dog walkers and farmers checking their flocks. This route became my retreat.

Summer

My parents, sister and I had great holidays in Cumbria like thousands of others.

The green fields look like a giant lawn. The old green trees in the valley mask the wild hilltops behind. After dawn in the early summer months, a grey-blue hue dusts the hillsides from the blue sky and grey stonework, and the emerging sun shows the orange and brown patches of life struggling high up the mountains. Each day of the year brings something new – a flower blooming for the first time in the year, a red squirrel's first season eating from a feeding station looking like a ball of fire.

A large oak tree by a footpath in the woodland near Aira Force gave me a brilliant view of this sleepy, mahogany tufted fur ball. We waited long enough to see it move to confirm we were looking at a red squirrel on a bed of moss and miniature ferns.

The summer sun blasting onto the fields and valleys below starts to dry the area. These arid patches are made worse when the clays and loams dry and crack, then the bogs and lake edges begin to flake and can erode more easily.

The long days of the summer solstice mean more chance to see badgers out and about in daylight. As the ground gets drier and harder, they scavenge around the village because they can't dig for worms and grubs.

My first evidence of badgers was finding bin bags ripped open and taken advantage of, then the uprooting of the garden for worms in the wetter spring. They did the same to the back fields. This coincided with me putting up cameras at different points around the area to catch video evidence. I discovered they were quite the animal for getting around!

The old coffin route between Ambleside and Grasmere offers a beautiful June walk, just sandwiched between Rydal Mount and Grasmere overlooking Rydal Water and Loughrigg Fell where, like William Wordsworth, you can 'wander lonely as a cloud'. The realities of the old coffin routes are less appealing; your stops are in exactly the places where the pallbearers stopped to catch their breath as they travelled to and from Grasmere in medieval times.

The Badger Bar Inn is a perfect place to rest for a while. They used to regularly have a badger feeding on the edge of the car park, although I didn't get to see it. After all the effort of visiting sites and setting up projects, I hadn't realised how close they were to me. The student house was nearly empty one week. The badgers were visiting the garden and I had been trying to catch them on camera. One night, my mate Tom startled me by coming to tell me there was a badger in the garden! It was feeding about two metres from our kitchen window. Result! The garden was at a window level and meant we were looking directly at a badger; it was the best hide I have ever had! I couldn't wait to tell my other mates and family. I set up the camera whilst it stayed dry enough for them to visit again and I was excited to tell my mates.

-●

The early morning silence of Rydal Water is only disturbed by the song of the wren as it begins to sing and calls out to its territory and beyond. To me the view is one of the most welcoming, with green and brown fields and trees stretching across before the season transforms into deeper, rich varieties of colours. Above this are the blue and grey mountains, with the sun hitting them and bouncing down to the valley.

I approached a farmer to ask for permission to use his land for my river surveying and photography. After just ten minutes of walking and recording, I heard the kingfisher. Territory is important to them and they guard their patch by patrolling up and down. Finding a few humans must have been annoying and the tiny blue jet went past, blasting out its call. During the survey I found an old nest site on a straight bank where overhanging trees and vegetation provided shelter. I'm not sure if the kingfisher nest was a success because I had missed out on their action.

There was so much life on this stretch of river; there

Mother duck 'Jemima' showing her ducklings how to find food on Rydal Water.

were no obvious pollutants and the water looked clear and healthy on the stone riverbed. The dipper and goosander were some of the important players on this stretch too.

From the Golden Rule pub you can see dozens of tourists heading upwards on foot, bike and in cars. The pub, with its vibrantly coloured flower baskets, classic ales and rustic appeal, is very popular with both locals and tourists. Rydal and Coniston Water glisten in the evening. I took a photo of Rydal Water with some ducklings learning to dig for shoreline snacks.

I often spent the day walking with my mates or running in the countryside here and built up a connection to the area that strengthened the longer I spent there observing its rich wildlife. By chance, I saw pied and spotted flycatchers. I never expected to see them there but the mix of coppice and wet meadows around the edges of traditional farmland can throw up some nice finds. The central belt and southern lakes are home to patches of rich woodland. I heard the 'teacher, teacher' call of a great tit alone somewhere in the canopy, and made out a willow warbler and wood warbler flitting about in the depths of the tree canopy.

Beatrix Potter has left a great legacy in this area. She had the wealth and determination to do something about what she believed in. Near Sawrey is a beautiful little village that she was involved with, and it keeps its character and charm to this day. Potter died at the age of seventy-seven in 1943, leaving nearly 4000 acres and fourteen farms to the National Trust to protect. Nearly a century after her purchases, these are places that my family and I could enjoy.

The things she painted and wrote about are characters of the Lakes that still give pleasure today. A foxglove knitted in against grey, weathered stone walls with duck-egg blue, curly lichens; rich green mosses and young ferns; the delicate bumblebee dancing around the flower heads; these are all just as Beatrix would have enjoyed them.

Looking across the fields as you head out of Ambleside.

Previous generations had tough lives and relied on hard graft to survive. To survive through the challenges, this generation will need that same grit even though this is now a place built on tourism, not farming as it was before. Luxury properties for the growing tourism industry sit by the waterfront at Windermere. Tourists pour in to well-known locations such as Bowness and Keswick. How closely do they relate to the surrounding landscape? Do they realise how much wildlife has been excluded by development?

The UK government needs to work with the organisations that push for more action to boost conservation work to fund quality habitat creation to reverse the decline in the natural world. I believe that some parts of the landscape should be re-formed or even partially abandoned; re-wilding could benefit the area as another source of tourism, showing the culture of the current day Lake District, like Ennerdale and Hardknott projects, before man chopped and changed them.

George Monbiot's comments about the sheep-wrecked landscape were honest and brutal, and World Heritage has stated its thoughts about striking a balance between nature and culture. The work to rebalance should promote local farming in the best ways, but should also recognise that not all farms are viable. Farming and forestry high up on the fells are surely going to change; revolutionary work is needed in a national park with a high profile that has recently been designated a UNESCO World Heritage site.

Raptors

Raptors have special significance in countries across the world, like the symbol of the eagle in Germany and the USA. Economically, birds of prey have been used in falconry to help catch food as is still the case in Central Asia. In more recent times, the protection of nest sites in the UK has provided opportunities for watch points like Symonds Yat Rock in Herefordshire, which attracts visitors who spend £500,000 in the Forest of Dean each year.

These beautiful animals are birds of prey or raptors. They are important for biodiversity and balancing the health of predator–prey relationships. In the British Isles there are diurnal and nocturnal groups. I would like to focus some attention on a couple of the daytime species that have provided me with surprise encounters. Sometimes I've driven hours to find them, then spent hours in front of my lens waiting for them; sometimes I've had to rush to grab and set up my camera before I miss the shot.

Raptors, like the buzzard, marsh harrier and white-tailed sea eagle, have faced persecution but they have bounced back. After habitat loss and persecution, the osprey, marsh harrier and red kite went into decline and have now started to repopulate areas they were forced to leave. Each of these species was on my list of birds to see.

●

Eagles dominate the sky. They are harassed by other scavengers as they glide and observe the landscape below. The golden eagle regularly takes sheep afterbirth, rabbits and larger prey such as young deer. They can stand as tall as a hill sheep, which explains why farmers are wary of them. Raptor species have been accused of being detrimental to an environment managed by man, and conservation battles against this attitude.

The last resident golden eagle in England was feared dead after disappearing in 2016. In Wales, an escapee golden eagle made its home in the Welsh Cambrian mountains, until sadly found dead in Powys in 2020. Both of these individuals, living out their days in the mountains and valleys, have shown that their species should be living on our isles; they can survive even when they become the only representatives of their species.

The small populations in Scotland may eventually repopulate these areas but, for now, I've missed my chance to connect with these eagles in England and Wales, though I have been lucky enough to see them in Scotland. Although a population could move out of southern Scotland over the border to England, it is feared this species may become a victim to wildlife crime and persecution.

In Ireland, just as the UK, the current reintroduction of a small population in Donegal is not having an easy ride, as habitat conditions are poor in parts of their former range. Food supplies are low and weather conditions hamper breeding. There is work to do for this species to become a more common sight in the valleys across the British Isles.

We currently have two projects in the UK. One is in the South of Scotland, which is aiming to support the remaining birds by relocating birds from more northern areas of the country to join residents in the southern uplands. The second project is in Snowdonia in Wales, where hopefully a viable project will begin soon.

⟡

Some hawks scavenge on decay in the countryside or hunt prey such as rabbits, worms and frogs. Hen harriers favour moorland; frustratingly, they are often persecuted because they can prey on young game birds raised for shoots. We have falcons too. Although they are the smallest, they are effective hunters, hard hitting with their speed and accuracy. The predator–prey relationship here is solid, with constant battles between peregrines and pigeons and likewise with hobby falcons and dragonflies.

To me, each bird is like a superhero of their habitat, at the top of their game, battling for meals against a prey which has evolved to outwit its pursuer. Our varied habitats are homes for birds like the osprey, also known as the river hawk or fish hawk. As its names suggest, the osprey provides its own unique way of hunting by catching fish, magnificently pulling them out of the water.

I saw my first osprey on the edge of Bassenthwaite Lake in Cumbria, a place they have nested successfully since 2001, the first recorded successful nesting since the 1830s in the Lake District. I asked my dad to stop the car near the lake. I got out and set up my lens, to scope the bird sitting on the bare bones of a dead tree. This bird, with its big beady eyes, was looking around the area it now calls home for part of the year.

At a Forestry Commission site nearby, I was able to take a look at their nest via a live stream camera set up to see from a distance. This bird, which migrates from Africa, had chosen to nest here on this lake. It looked very exotic with its stylish white and brown feathers and crest. It is slowly but surely expanding its range and taking the opportunity to breed in the UK once again.

I get a buzz every time I look up at the sky and see the silhouette of a red kite. Gliding and soaring in the bright sky, circling on the thermals, this is something I see every week now. The red kite is a species that was so heavily persecuted in the United Kingdom that it was pushed to the brink of extinction, with just a few of them surviving in Wales.

It is a credit to conservation work and an inspiration that such projects can be successful. Working in the Wiltshire countryside, I could see them all day long. They have really flourished and become a beautiful addition to the skies. You can hear their call and know the chances of seeing them are good. In my workplace I often get asked if a bird in the sky is a kite – people are still not sure what they are seeing. I sometimes get asked if they will eat the animals in my care, but there is plenty of food for them nearby, especially where the big cats are fed.

The easy way to identify this bird is by looking at its forked tail. It has a beautiful red and brown wing with a hint of cream and gold on the upper side of the wing. My Collins guide to identifying birds is a close companion; it was a gift before I went to university and I have treasured it ever since. It describes the red kite as medium sized to large and often long winged, which is exactly what I see. With a wingspan ranging from 1.4 to 1.8 metres, any flapping is going to take some effort, which is why they fly on the thermals and glide up high. The wings are angled like pointed, upside-down V shapes. This bird has slow, powerful movements in the sky; it saves energy by flowing with thermals and moving with the direction of the wind. Windy days make the kites look as if they enjoy being in the sky.

From Shakespeare's work, we know that London was a city of kites and crows. From a time when people were hung and left in the streets, or the population flung scraps out to reduce litter in the home, the kites would soar above, taking their opportunity where they could. Kites were useful in England and Wales to keep streets clean of carrion and food from rotting, but suddenly the word 'vermin' was added to this species and it resulted in them being killed.

In 1859, the last kite was reportedly seen in London. As we started tidying up the countryside, pests were managed by means of shooting and poisoning. Improvements to agricultural efficiency removed habitats, and kite numbers dropped nationwide in the twentieth century. Kite eggs became a prize for egg collectors, which drove down the numbers further to about forty pairs. To protect these birds, scoping out and protecting their nest sites stalled the activities of egg collectors; under the Protection of Birds Act of 1954 it became illegal to take birds' eggs from nests, and in 1982 it became illegal to possess new eggs. Kites survived in Wales and a project was started just in the nick of time to revive their numbers.

The species had what it needed to thrive: a landscape, food and shelter with no other kites. As many as fifty sightings a week have been reported in London this year; it is becoming a bird of the capital city once again. Driving on the M3, I saw kites high up in the autumn sun, back where they belong.

Kites were taken to Wales to boost bloodlines and ranges, and reintroduction in Northern Ireland, Northampton and Cumbria were all successful. I saw my first red kite in Grizedale, in Hawkshead of all places (mind the pun!). The thermals were high so the kites stayed up and soared down, calling out in the summer sunshine. A television programme showed UK farmers feeding red kites in order to benefit from their presence; a tourist boom was linked to the option of feeding these animals and has probably contributed to the breeding programme. In the

The glorious red kite in the skies above.

late 1980s, a number of kites were relocated to England and Scotland from Europe and both groups began to breed in 1992. Further releases joined populations in the South of England, Wales and Scotland. In the north-east of England, it was 2004. They are something I remember seeing as a kid and I hope that it will not be too many more years before I get to see them fly over my home area again. In 2019, a few individuals explored the edges of the moors and the Tees valley, which is exciting. It can be only a matter of time before I see them regularly.

My second sighting was a trip past the renowned Angel of the North; strangely enough, the statue's wings stretch out like the kite and it is a rich iron-brown colour too. I was on my way to the National Trust site at Gibside, Gateshead, to a landscape where kites have been reintroduced and are now breeding. The National Trust site is not far away from the city. The area comprises access for the red kites over to the Pennines, the old mining areas, farmland and towns. We were close to the National Trust managed estate near Gateshead and I was looking out of the window for brown tourist signs. We got a bit off track and ended up on a street opposite hedges and fields. That was when I saw the kite, within metres of the car.

The kite was searching along the hedge line and field margins for some grub. It was very low and, probably because we were in a slow-moving car, it was in no hurry as it searched the field boundaries. In the distance we could see the centre of Newcastle. The kite's large eyes sat in the centre of its head, and it had a vibrant yellow gape and grey flecked head. The markings are stunning. I didn't see any kites at Gibside but not to worry; I got a new life tick, a close encounter with a wild raptor, a family day out, and we saw a pair of buzzards circling high above the estate monument.

I know that stories of kites taking rabbits and chickens have worried people. I met a lady who said her little 'chooks' were fearful of low-flying kites. Some individuals are still cautious about animals and birds being brought back that were previously removed for people's benefit. Sadly, I read a report stating the estimated survival of Scottish red kites in the 1990s was only two-thirds of their number, the final third being a victim to illegal poisoning. Poisoned animals – usually mice, rats, foxes and crows – are taken by birds in England, only for them to fall victim to the poison too.

One project was to create a self-sustaining population of red kites on the outskirts of Aberdeen, of which the people of Aberdeen can be proud of and enjoy.

The bird that I write about makes a weekly appearance in the sky and always makes me smile. I am pleased and proud to enjoy sharing the landscape with this scavenger bird of the thermals in the twenty-first century after the threat of extinction that we put them under.

The black kite is a species that searches for food on the northern coasts of France; occasionally they are blown or fly across to UK waters and about twenty-five are spotted every year. These kites may see potential new homes across the Channel; perhaps they will breed here as the climate changes which would be a lovely addition to the landscape. On a similar note, I was very excited when a video emerged of the white-tailed sea eagle, the largest of the UK birds of prey, flying around the skies of southern England being harassed by a red kite. This species is being trialled for reintroduction in England. After success in Scotland, fingers crossed it may be here to stay. Seeing them alongside the red kite makes you realise that conservation efforts can have positive effects if they correctly carried out.

Conservation and Our Connections

ONE SCHOOL HOLIDAY when I was about fifteen, I started a mini-science experiment at home. I was examining behavioural responses in feral pigeons. My test was to find out what makes the birds alert. Could I get their survival instincts to show straight away and record them?

At that age, I didn't know much about science. I started in the garden with the calls of three possible predators: the buzzard, kestrel and sparrowhawk. The first made the pigeons stop feeding; the second made them alert, and the sparrowhawk was enough to make the pigeons fly off.

To check that they weren't just being nervous that I was playing predator calls at certain times, as a control I played a pop song. This, too, made them look alert, showing that the feral pigeons respond to both familiar and non-familiar sounds with caution.

Animals, birds and places have always held a fascination for me. I am not alone in this; eagle watching on the Isle of Mull and seeing red kites soaring are just some of the things I've done that you can do too.

We are making progress in conservation and re-populating animal and bird communities. Raptors are returning to our skies; work is being undertaken to restore reed beds. We are moving in the right direction. I have read about Peterborough Council cutting their grass fewer times to save cash and help wildlife, and there have been similar schemes in my home town where mini-meadows are valuable additions. A recent push for bee highway habitats is one method that could be adopted everywhere. We cannot let those in charge destroy the preservation and recovery of natural communities. If something needs to change, surely it can be done with the help of a community and funding.

The effects of the pandemic lockdown in 2020 have given nature a bounce, and we've begun to see small changes. At home our camera traps captured visiting fox cubs and hedgehogs. At work this spring, I was in search of fresh grass to feed animals. Normally, I would walk right past this particular spot at the lake edge but with no time pressure to get from A to B, I noticed how vibrant and buzzing this little patch was. A transformation had happened in the three months of spring. I looked at three patches within the one space that had developed differently due to the amount of sunlight they received. This environment had been left to its own devices. Any work that would normally have been done had stopped because of lockdown.

In the centre was lush grass with mares' tail, and to the right were daisies and purple bugle and other flowers under a tree.

To the left was a larger tree, more shaded, with butter-cups and forget-me-nots in the grass around it. A few hairy-looking grasses under the tree were sprinkled with bird droppings that showed evidence of the cereals that are fed to the animals nearby. The connection between animals and birds was easy to see; they live amongst each other and with us – yet we have been detaching ourselves from them.

As I've been writing, my own feeling of connection to nature has continued to grow. Like any project you get involved with, it comes to the forefront of your everyday life. I started writing about my experiences in connecting to the natural world; as I wrote this book, I became even more excited by the links I could pull together.

I found myself looking into the distance, listening and watching life, just as I did when I was younger. The visits to national parks, reserves and estates as a kid allowed me to explore animals, birds and landscapes. We need to work hard now to cherish these places. Volunteering and visits will not only help the conservation organisations, they could help you too.

The way we work and live is often at the expense of nature, but it becomes expensive or time consuming to repair the damage when things go wrong. In the UK, many native species have been persecuted and hunted to extinction in the past. How can we expect other nations to preserve the Sumatran tiger, the monarch butterfly and the black rhino when we can't even save what is left on our islands?

We are often blind to the natural world around us and

think that 'real' nature is far away in tropical countries. We should preserve and enhance what we have locally. National parks, reserves and gardens are some of the richest habitats we have left and provide nature with an array of places to live and visit. We must make sure they are maintained and connected so that wildlife can travel easily to other similar places. That way, we can continue to connect with nature. Let's hope the work in the next decade can repair more of our countryside.

Me and my friend Michael looking for Red deer in Cumbria.

Image: © Tom Parker

End Notes

I WAS NEVER any good at reading or writing, so it feels like a massive achievement to have written this book.

My first twenty-five years have been interesting. I didn't expect to be away from friends and family walking in the sunny south-west of England during a worldwide pandemic. Thank goodness for the natural world.

I hope you have enjoyed my stories and connected with my joy in nature. My chance to interact with the environment has changed me, and I am forever learning and zoning in to another world. Nature captivates me and provides escape.

Each day wildlife fight for survival: often against the actions of man. If wildlife is allowed a healthy amount of time and space, it can be sustainable in the same way that we can be.

I look forward to finding future connections.

Acknowledgements

To be able to be outside and explore nature is something special for me: nature is amazing. One of the great things I picked up from writing this book was how it helped complete a picture. I 'saw' memories and it created opportunities to think and reflect.

I am thankful for being able to share my story; my own perspective on the world I have experienced.

There are many people I have to thank for allowing me to follow my passion and for being part of my journey. Far too many to mention here, but without your encouragement and support I wouldn't be who I am. I will always be grateful. Thank you.

I would like to mention my Dad, Mam and Beth. I'm sure I've driven you mad at times, but this life and passion I've been able to follow has allowed me to flourish. We've had lots of adventures and I'm sure there will be more to come. I want to thank you for your daily support, dedication and encouragement in whatever I do, from getting up early and out the house, to helping with research and taking care of all the animals. I really do appreciate you.

Thank you, Chloe, for all you do and for all the adventures yet to come.

To my friends, I might not see you all the time but I am grateful for your friendship. Thank you to the farming people (in particular, Mr Murray) for sharing your time, experiences and your way of life with me.

Thank you to the staff and volunteers at RSPB Saltholme for your encouragement and helping me to continue my growth… well I'm pretty much the same size. To Volker, for your supervision when stepping up to academic work.

And finally thank you to the team at 2QT Publishing for your care in helping me to transform my writing into this book. Thank you to Catherine, Hilary, Karen and artist Emmy for all your contributions.

Lightning Source UK Ltd.
Milton Keynes UK
UKHW020416130721
387045UK00007B/353